Bach for an Encore

Menu classics

"The wine of Love is music,
And the feast of Love is song:
And when Love sits down to the banquet,
Love sits long . . . "

Published by
THE JUNIOR COMMITTEE OF
THE CLEVELAND ORCHESTRA
Severance Hall
Cleveland, Ohio 44106

to Benefit
THE CLEVELAND ORCHESTRA

First Printing — 20,000 copies — May 1983

ISBN 0-9609142-2-6

For additional copies of BACH FOR AN ENCORE: Menu Classics, BACH'S LUNCH: Picnic and Patio Classics, or BACH FOR MORE: Fireside Classics, use the order blank in the back of this book, or write to:

BACH COOKBOOKS
Severance Hall
Cleveland, Ohio 44106

Check should be made payable to Bach Cookbooks in the amount of $6.95 plus $1.50 for postage and handling per book. Ohio delivery please add $.46 sales tax per book.

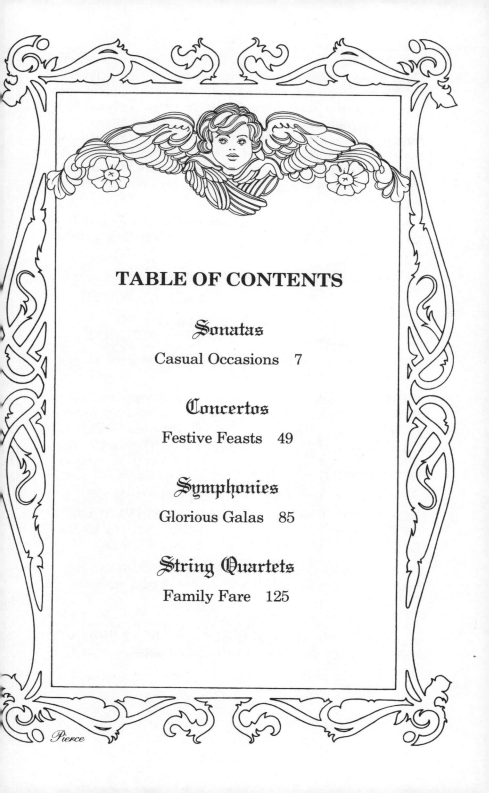

TABLE OF CONTENTS

Sonatas

Concertos

Symphonies

String Quartets

Pierce

BACH FOR AN ENCORE — The third of the Bach Series Cookbooks, published for the benefit of The Cleveland Orchestra, is a unique offering of menu selections for entertaining on any scale from family to forty. Its appearance would not have been possible without the support of our hundreds of recipe contributors. Unfortunately, space did not permit us to include all of the fine recipes received. To standardize measurements and procedures, editorial adjustments have been made — we expect these will meet with the approval of the contributors.

Plan an adventure and let your mood find a menu to match. We know that your guests will enjoy your interpretation of these classic themes.

Bon Appetit!

Chairman:	NANCY L. WALSH
Co-Editors:	SARA HAWK
	LINDA KRESNYE

Special thanks to the entire Cookbook Committee who gave untold hours of time and talent:

BRENDA K. ASHLEY	*Publication Chairman*
BONNIE FEMEC	*Design Chairman*
DIANE M. GILL	*Publication Chairman*
CAROLYN ROSS	*Testing Chairman*
MARY ANNE SCHMITZ	*Data Processing Chairman*
DIANNE VOGT	*Collection Chairman*

CHRISTINE AMBROSE	DIANE HENNESSEY
VIRGINIA BARBATO	KATHERINE MAVEC
CONNIE A. BUKVIC	CHRISTINE M. ULRICH
KATHLEEN GRIFFIN	RENA WIDZER

All recipes submitted to **BACH FOR AN ENCORE** have been tested by our testers and reviewed and edited by the Committee.

For your enjoyment, we have included wine suggestions where appropriate. We are most grateful to PAT O'BRIEN for sharing his expertise in providing the selections.

Sonatas

Casual Occasions

Pierce

"SNOW MAIDEN"

*Stuffed Artichoke Bottoms
*Honey-Mustard Pork Roast
*Noodle-Rice Pilaf
Buttered Beets
*Walnut Raisin Spice Cake with
Cream Cheese Frosting
German Rhine Spatlese

STUFFED ARTICHOKE BOTTOMS

12 artichoke bottoms
½ lb. small shrimp
4 T. butter
½ lb. mushrooms, chopped
1 T. white wine
salt and pepper to taste
1 cup chicken stock
1 tsp. cornstarch
½ cup sour cream
dill for garnish

Melt butter over medium heat. Stir in chopped mushrooms, wine, salt and freshly ground pepper. Simmer 3 to 4 minutes covered. Heat the chicken stock. Mix cornstarch with sour cream, add it to the boiling chicken stock and cook for 1 minute. Arrange artichoke bottoms on four plates. Place the shrimp on the bottoms, then pour stock and mushroom mixtures over. Garnish with dill.

Serves 4   ANTAL DORATI

HONEY-MUSTARD PORK ROAST

5 to 6 lbs. center-cut pork roast
1 clove minced garlic
1 tsp. thyme
3 to 4 T. honey-mustard
1 T. flour
3 T. orange or lemon marmalade
salt and pepper to taste
¼ to ½ cup cider, apple juice or
   white wine

Mix garlic, thyme, honey-mustard, flour, marmalade, salt and pepper and spread on roast. Cook 25 minutes per pound at 325 degrees. Approximately 30 to 35 minutes from start of cooking, add some of the cider or wine. Keep adding as it evaporates and cooks. Remove roast and let stand 15 minutes or so with a tent of foil placed loosely over it before slicing. Scrape pan drippings with a non-metallic spatula and use for gravy.

Serves 4   PAT DE FABIO SHIMRAK

NOODLE-RICE PILAF

4 oz. fine noodles
1 cup rice
1 stick butter, melted
1 small can chicken bouillon
1 cup water
onion salt and white pepper to taste

Saute uncooked noodles in butter. Watch carefully, stirring to golden brown. Add rice, bouillon, and water, cooking until tender. Season to taste.

Serves 5   PAULA KAPPOS

WALNUT RAISIN SPICE CAKE WITH CREAM CHEESE FROSTING

1½ cups raisins
1½ cups walnuts
1½ tsp. baking soda
1½ cups boiling water
¾ cup butter
1½ cups sugar
2 whole eggs
2 egg yolks
2¼ cups sifted all-purpose flour
1½ tsp. lemon juice
¼ tsp. salt
1½ tsp. cinnamon
1½ tsp. vanilla

Grease and flour three 8-inch round cake pans. Finely chop raisins and walnuts, add soda and boiling water; cool 30 minutes. Sift flour, cinnamon, and salt; set aside. Beat butter until creamy. Slowly add sugar, beating until light and fluffy. Add eggs and egg yolks one at a time, beating after each addition. Add lemon juice and vanilla. Add flour mixture in fourths alternating with raisin-nut mixture in thirds. Bake at 350 degrees for 25 to 30 minutes. After baking, cool for 5 minutes. Loosen edges and turn onto racks to cool. Frost with Cream Cheese Frosting.

CREAM CHEESE FROSTING

1-8 oz. pkg. cream cheese, softened
⅔ cup margarine
3 tsp. vanilla
1½ lbs. confectioners' sugar

Blend margarine and cream cheese. Add remaining ingredients and mix well.

Serves 12 to 16   CHRISTINA THOBURN

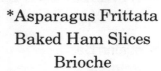

"RITES OF SPRING"
*Asparagus Frittata
Baked Ham Slices
Brioche
*French Glacé Strawberry Pie
Macon Lugny

ASPARAGUS FRITTATA

6 eggs
1 large onion, sliced
½ lb. asparagus, in 2-inch lengths
salt and pepper
¼ cup good olive oil or vegetable oil

Saute onion and asparagus in oil 12 minutes. Mix eggs thoroughly with fork. Pour over vegetables. Move egg mixture from edge of pan allowing oil to seep through eggs. When eggs are three-fourths cooked, slide frittata out of pan onto dish. Invert pan over dish and return to heat, to finish cooking for 1 minute.

Serves 4 to 6   PAT DeFABIO SHIMRAK

FRENCH GLACÉ STRAWBERRY PIE

1 pre-baked cooled pie shell
3 oz. pkg. cream cheese
1 qt. strawberries
1 cup sugar
3 T. cornstarch

Spread cream cheese on shell. Wash, drain and hull berries. Cover shell with three-fourths of berries. Mash remaining berries until juice is extracted. If necessary, add water to make 1½ cups juice. Bring to boiling and gradually stir in sugar mixed with cornstarch. Cook over low heat, stirring constantly until thickened. Cool. Pour over berries in shell. Chill. Serve with whipped cream.

Serves 6 to 8   NANCY L. WALSH

AFTER THE CATCH DINNER

Catch of the Day
*Beer Batter
Cornsticks
Broccoli with Lemon
*Crisp Ginger Cookies with Sliced Peaches
or
*Sandwich Cookies
Rhone White or Macon Lugny

BEER BATTER FOR FISH, SHRIMP, FRUITS OR VEGETABLES

**2 cups flour
½ tsp. salt
12 oz. beer
3 egg whites, beaten until soft peaks
    form
2 cups oil**

Combine flour, salt and beer. Mix well (it will be firm). Stir in a small amount of beaten egg whites to lighten mixture, then fold in rest thoroughly. Heat oil in deep pot to 375 degrees. Dip fish into batter and drop in oil. Fry until puffed and golden. Batter can be stored, refrigerated, 2 to 3 days.

GINNA HERMANN

SANDWICH COOKIES

5 cups flour
1 cup butter
1 cup shortening
4 egg yolks
4 T. sour cream
1 cup + 2 T. sugar
2 tsp. baking powder
2 tsp. vanilla
1-18 oz. jar red raspberry preserves
confectioners' sugar

Mix all ingredients except for preserves. Roll dough on sugared board. Cut out cookies with small cutter. Using a thimble, cut center holes in half of the cookies. Bake on ungreased sheets at 375 degrees for 10 to 20 minutes. Cool, spread bottom cookie with preserves. Top with cookie with hole. Dust with confectioners' sugar.

Yield: 12 dozen   LINDA KRESNYE

CRISP GINGER COOKIES

4 cups sifted flour
½ cup sugar
½ tsp. baking soda
2½ to 3 tsp. ginger
1 tsp. cinnamon
2 cups butter
1¼ cups warm molasses

Sift flour, sugar, soda, ginger, and cinnamon. Cut in the butter until consistency of crumbs. Stir in warm molasses and mix quickly. Cover and chill. When stiff divide dough in half and shape into rolls 1½ inches in diameter. Wrap and refrigerate or freeze. Slice thin and bake at 350 degrees for 10 minutes.

Yield: 4 to 6 dozen   MRS. HAROLD ENSTEN

"PRIMAVERA CONCERTO"

*Budapest Canape
*Linguine Primavera Salad
or
*Ratatouille Pie
Crusty French Bread
*Frozen White Chocolate Mousse
Nuits St. George or Hermitage Blanc

BUDAPEST CANAPE

**1 loaf bread
butter
anchovy butter
hard-cooked eggs
paprika
watercress**

Cut bread into ⅓-inch slices. Shape into crescents, and saute in butter until delicately browned. Spread with anchovy butter and set aside. Separate whites and yolks of eggs. Chop whites and season with paprika. Set aside. Force yolks through sieve. Sprinkle half of crescents with egg white and other half with yolk. Garnish with sprigs of watercress.

MRS. ZOLTAN GOMBOS

LINGUINE PRIMAVERA SALAD

- 1 lb. linguine, al dente
- 1 cup broccoli florets, steamed 3 minutes
- 1 cup carrots, sliced, steamed 5 minutes
- 1 cup zucchini, sliced
- 1 cup mushrooms, sliced
- ¼ lb. ham, minced
- ½ of 16-oz. can small pitted black olives, drained
- ½ cup pecans
- ¼ cup Parmesan cheese, grated
- ¼ cup Romano cheese, freshly grated

Marinate linguine in half of vinaigrette salad dressing and refrigerate overnight. Add remaining ingredients using as much salad dressing as is necessary to coat all. Refrigerate several hours and toss right before serving. Garnish with extra cheese and nuts.

VINAIGRETTE DRESSING

- 1½ cups olive oil
- ½ cup shallot vinegar or white wine vinegar
- 2 cloves garlic, pressed
- 1 cup green onions, sliced
- ¼ cup parsley, minced
- 2 T. fresh oregano, chopped or 2 tsp. dried
- 2 T. fresh basil, chopped
- 1 tsp. sea salt
- freshly ground pepper

Combine dressing in screw-top jar. Congeals when refrigerated. Bring to room temperature before using.

Serves 8   CARYL HALLE

RATATOUILLE PIE

1 lb. eggplant, peeled and cubed
2 zucchini, scrubbed and cubed
1 onion, chopped
4 tomatoes, peeled, seeded and
    chopped
¼ cup olive oil
½ tsp. basil
3 eggs
¼ cup Parmesan cheese
1 tsp. parsley
½ tsp. oregano
¼ lb. mozzarella cheese

Saute eggplant in oil. Add onion and unpeeled, cubed zucchini. Cook 10 minutes covered or until vegetables are soft. Add tomatoes. Cook about 15 more minutes. Let cool. Beat eggs. Add Parmesan cheese, basil, parsley, oregano and pepper. Add mixture to vegetables. Butter a 9-inch or 10-inch pie pan and pour in one-half of mixture. Sprinkle with Parmesan. Add remaining mixture, sprinkle with more Parmesan and mozzarella cheese. Bake at 400 degrees 40 minutes or until set.

Serves 6   KATIE LORETTA

FROZEN
WHITE CHOCOLATE MOUSSE

8 oz. chocolate wafer cookies
3 T. sweet butter, melted
½ tsp. cinnamon
½ cup boiling water
12 oz. white chocolate, coarsely chopped
4 eggs, extra large, separated
3 cups whipping cream
pinch of salt
½ tsp. cream of tartar
¾ cup sugar

Preheat oven to 375 degrees. Separate 9-inch spring-form pan. Butter sides only. Reassemble and set aside. Pulverize cookies and cinnamon in food processor. Pour crumbs into a bowl and stir in butter. Pour two-thirds mixture into pan. Press crumbs against sides. Press remaining crumbs over bottom of pan. Bake at 375 degrees 7 to 8 minutes. Remove from oven, cool and set aside. Over low heat melt chocolate with boiling water. Stir until smooth. Remove from heat and cool slightly. Whisk in egg yolks, one at a time. Cool mixture completely. Whip cream until it holds shape. Set aside. Beat egg whites until foamy. Add salt and cream of tartar. Beat until soft peaks form. Gradually add sugar and continue beating until stiff but not dry. Fold chocolate into egg whites. Then fold together whipped cream and chocolate mixture. Pour into crust. Freeze for 1 hour before covering. Cover and freeze at least 5 hours or more, or overnight. May be frozen up to 2 weeks. Serve with whipped cream, chocolate leaves or chocolate-covered strawberries.

Serves 8 to 10   ALYCE HOBBS

SOUTH OF THE BORDER

*Tex-Mex Dip
*Tank Flank
*My Mom's Zucchini Casserole
Sesame Sticks
*Fruit Pizza
or
*Blueberry Pie
California Barbera or Gigondas

TEX-MEX DIP

**3 medium ripe avocados
2 T. lemon juice
½ tsp. salt
¼ tsp. pepper
1 cup (8 oz.) sour cream
½ cup mayonnaise
1 package taco seasoning mix
2 cans Jalapeno Bean Dip
1 cup green onions, chopped
3 medium tomatoes, chopped
    (2 cups)
2-3½ oz. cans chopped black olives
    (drained)
1-8 oz. package shredded cheddar
    cheese
large tortilla chips**

Peel, pit, mash avocados in medium bowl with lemon juice, salt and pepper. Combine sour cream, mayonnaise and taco seasoning. Spread bean dip on large platter. Top with avocado mixture, then sour cream-taco mixture. Sprinkle with green onions, tomatoes, olives. Cover with cheese. Refrigerate until serving. Serve with chips.

Serves 12   BARBARA WILSON

TANK FLANK

2 to 2½ lbs. flank steak
⅔ cup soy sauce
⅔ cup chutney
⅔ cup oil
⅔ cup red wine
1 T. minced onion
2 cloves garlic, minced
Sauce:
¾ cup mayonnaise
¼ cup horseradish

Pierce steak all over with fork. Mix soy sauce, chutney, oil, wine and garlic and marinate 12 to 24 hours. Grill or broil steak to desired doneness. Slice thinly against grain of meat. Mix mayonnaise and horseradish and serve on side.

Serves 4 to 6   SALLY DeROULET

MY MOM'S ZUCCHINI CASSEROLE

4 cups zucchini, sliced
1 large onion, chopped
½ cup green pepper, chopped
1½ T. flour
1 T. brown sugar, packed
2 cups stewed tomatoes
grated cheese — swiss, cheddar
    or Parmesan
4 T. butter

Slice zucchini and place in a greased baking dish. Saute onion and pepper in 4 T. butter until soft. Add flour, mix well. Add sugar and stewed tomatoes and cook over low heat until thickened, stirring often. Pour on top of zucchini and mix gently. Bake 45 to 60 minutes at 350 degrees. Sprinkle cheese on top the last 15 minutes of baking.

Serves 6   HELEN GREENLEAF

FRUIT PIZZA

½ cup melted butter
1 cup flour
2 T. sugar
1-8 oz. package cream cheese
⅓ cup sugar
1 tsp. vanilla
4 kinds of fruit, fresh or canned
   (drain the canned fruit well)
½ cup marmalade

Mix together melted butter, flour and sugar. Pat into a 10-inch pizza pan and bake at 375 degrees for 10 to 15 minutes or until golden brown. Blend softened cream cheese with sugar and vanilla. Spread on cooled crust. Arrange fruit "artfully" on top. Suggested fruits are: fresh seeded grapes, kiwi, blueberries, plums, cherries, bananas, peaches, strawberries. Then top with glaze: heat ½ cup marmalade and bit of water. Cool. Then pour over fruit.

Serves 6   NANCY GAGE

BLUEBERRY PIE

1 10-inch unbaked pie crust
pastry for lattice top
3 pints fresh blueberries (clean,
   check for stems)
1½ cups sugar
⅓ cup flour
1 to 2 tsp. cinnamon
butter

Heat oven to 425 degrees. Stir together sugar, flour and cinnamon. Add blueberries and mix. Pour into unbaked crust. Add dots of butter. Cover with lattice top. Bake at 425 degrees for 45 to 50 minutes.

Serves 6 to 8   FRAN BUCKLEY

SCRUMPTIOUS BRUNCH

*The Great Puffy Pancake
Canadian Bacon Slices
Fresh Fruit with
*Currant and Cheese Dressing
*Orange Caramel Custard
Bernkastler Riesling Kabinett

THE GREAT PUFFY PANCAKE

½ cup flour
½ cup milk
2 eggs, slightly beaten
pinch nutmeg
4 T. butter
2 T. confectioners' sugar
juice of ½ lemon

Preheat oven to 425 degrees. Mix flour, eggs, milk and nutmeg together, leaving batter a bit lumpy. Melt butter in large frying pan and add the batter. Bake 15 to 20 minutes until golden brown. Sprinkle with confectioners' sugar and return to oven briefly. Sprinkle with lemon juice. Cut into wedges. This can easily be doubled and put into 9 x 13-inch glass dish.

Serves 4   DOROTHY BERGOINE

CURRANT AND CHEESE DRESSING

4 oz. cream cheese
1 T. lemon juice
2 oz. currant jelly
¼ cup cream

Mix all ingredients until smooth.

Serves 4 to 6   CHARLOTTE JACKSON

ORANGE CARAMEL CUSTARD

¾ cup sugar
¼ cup water
pinch cream of tartar
1½ cups milk
½ cup heavy cream
3 eggs
2 egg yolks
⅓ cup sugar
¼ cup strained orange juice
1 T. orange liqueur
1 tsp. grated orange rind
thin strips of orange peel

In heavy skillet combine sugar, water and cream of tartar. Heat mixture over moderately low heat, stirring and washing down any sugar crystals clinging to the sides of pan with brush dipped in cold water, until sugar is dissolved. Cook mixture over moderate heat undisturbed until it turns a deep caramel. Pour caramel into four ¾-cup ramekins, coating the bottoms evenly. In saucepan, scald milk and heavy cream. In a bowl beat whole eggs, egg yolks and sugar until mixture is just combined. Add hot milk in a stream, stirring, then add strained orange juice and liqueur. Skim froth from the surface, stir in grated orange rind and pour mixture into ramekins. Set ramekins in baking pan, pour enough hot water to reach halfway up the sides of ramekins. Bake custards, covered with a baking sheet, in a preheated 325 degree oven for 25 to 30 minutes, or until they are almost set. Remove the custards from the baking pan, cool and chill covered, overnight. Release the edges of the custards from the ramekins with a knife, invert a dessert plate over each ramekin, and invert onto plates. Top the custards with very thin strips of orange peel which have been blanched in boiling water for 1 minute then well drained.

Serves 4   PAULA KAPPOS

APRÈS SKI

*Lentil Soup
Pumpernickel Bread with
Sweet Butter
*Peach Cheese Pie

LENTIL SOUP

A piece of smoked meat or a ham
  bone
1 package of lentils (rinsed and
  picked over)
½ cup diced celery
1 grated clove garlic (optional)
1 tsp. salt
2 quarts cold water
1 cup tomato juice
1 finely chopped onion
1 bay leaf
⅛ tsp. pepper
3 garlic sausages, sliced
1 T. bacon fat
1 T. flour
vinegar (optional)

If using smoked meat, cook for one hour in water.
Add lentils, celery, garlic, salt, water, tomato juice,
onion, bay leaf and pepper. Cook slowly for 1½
hours. Chill. Remove meat and bone. Skim fat from
the pan. Fry garlic sausage (knockers) lightly in
bacon fat. Add to soup. Remove all but 1 T. fat from
pan. Add flour and some of soup gradually. Mix with
remaining soup. Season. A touch of vinegar may be
added. Serve hot. If too thick, add water.

Serves 6   MRS. FRANK E. JOSEPH, SR.

PEACH CHEESE PIE

¾ cup flour
1 tsp. baking powder
½ tsp. salt
1 package dry vanilla pudding mix
  (not instant)
3 T. butter
1 egg
½ cup milk
1-15 to 20 oz. can sliced peaches in
  heavy syrup
½ cup sugar
8 oz. cream cheese
3 T. reserved peach syrup
2 T. sugar
cinnamon

Combine flour, baking powder, salt, vanilla pudding, butter, egg and milk. Pour into greased pie plate. Drain peaches, reserve syrup. Pour into pie plate. Cream sugar, cream cheese and reserved syrup. Spoon over peaches. Sprinkle with cinnamon and sugar. Bake at 350 degrees for 30 minutes.

Serves 6 to 8   FRAN BUCKLEY

"POLONAISE"

*Quick and Easy Marinated Mushrooms
*Baked Chicken Mary Jane
*Swope Bread
*Old Dominion Pound Cake with Fresh Fruit
Chateauneuf Du Pape or California Zinfandel

QUICK AND EASY MARINATED MUSHROOMS

2/3 cup vinegar
1/2 cup olive oil (be sure to use olive oil)
2 cloves garlic (optional)
1 tsp. sugar
1 1/2 tsp. salt
1 1/2 tsp. oregano
1 to 1 1/2 tsp. pepper
2 T. water
1 medium Bermuda onion, sliced in rings
1 quart mushrooms, cleaned with larger ones halved lengthwise

Place onions and mushrooms in large plastic container with tight fitting top. Combine all other ingredients in blender; mix for a few seconds. Pour over mushrooms and onions. Store refrigerated up to two weeks. Invert every few days.

BARBARA SILVERS

BAKED CHICKEN MARY JANE

1 cup sour cream
2 tsp. soy sauce
½ tsp. garlic salt
2 T. lemon juice
1 tsp. celery salt
1 tsp. paprika
dash of pepper
1 small pkg. herb-seasoned stuffing
   crumbs
3 split chicken breasts, skinned and
   boned
melted butter

Mix together sour cream, soy sauce, garlic salt, lemon juice, celery salt, paprika, and pepper. Dip chicken into mixture and then roll in the seasoned bread crumbs. Arrange pieces in a lightly greased baking dish. Drizzle them with melted butter and bake uncovered at 325 degrees for 1 hour.

Serves 4   ANN CICARELLA

SWOPE BREAD

1 cup flour
2 cups whole wheat flour
½ cup sugar
1 tsp. salt
2 cups buttermilk
2 tsp. baking soda

Mix flours, sugar and salt together. Combine buttermilk and baking soda, add to flour. Mix thoroughly. Pour in greased 9 x 5-inch loaf pan. Bake at 350 degrees for 1 hour and 10 minutes.

MRS. ROBERT GARDNER

OLD DOMINION POUNDCAKE

8 or 10 large eggs, separated
2¼ cups sifted all-purpose flour
¼ tsp. baking soda
1¼ cups granulated sugar
1½ cups butter, softened
2 T. fresh lemon juice
2¼ tsp. vanilla extract
⅛ tsp. salt
1 cup granulated sugar
1½ tsp. cream of tartar

Make day before serving. Let eggs stand at room temperature 1 hour before using. Meanwhile, butter well and flour a 10-inch bundt pan. Sift together flour, soda and 1¼ cups sugar. Preheat oven to 325 degrees. In large bowl, with mixer at low speed, just barely blend butter with flour mixture, then add lemon juice and vanilla. Beat in egg yolks, one at a time, just until blended. Beat egg whites at high speed until frothy. Add salt; then gradually add 1 cup sugar mixed with cream of tartar. Beat well after each addition and continue beating until soft peaks form. Gently fold beaten egg whites into cake batter and turn into the prepared pan. Then, using a rubber spatula, gently cut through the cake batter one or two times. Bake at 325 degrees, 1½ hours or until cake tester inserted in center comes out clean. (Do not peek at cake during first hour of baking.) Turn off oven heat; let cake remain in oven 15 minutes then remove to wire cake rack and cool 15 minutes more. Remove cake from pan, finish cooling on rack. Wrap in foil or store in cake box until served.

Serves 24   MRS. JAMES A. WOLF

*Cold Cucumber Soup with Dill
*Fish en Papillot
*Tomatoes Stuffed with Vermicelli
*Oranges Filled with Fruits
*Chocolate Macaroons
California Chardonnay or Mersault

COLD CUCUMBER SOUP WITH DILL

**4 green onions with tops, sliced
4 T. unsalted butter
4 baking potatoes, peeled and sliced
thinly
6 to 8 cups chicken stock skimmed
of fat
2 T. dill weed
1½ cups milk
2 cups sour cream
2 medium cucumbers, peeled,
sliced, and diced
chives
salt and pepper**

Saute onions in butter; add potatoes and stock. Bring to a boil, then simmer for 15 minutes. Cool and puree in blender. Add dill, milk and sour cream. Chill. Add cucumbers. Let flavors "marry" for a few hours or overnight. Serve with a sprinkling of chives, salt, and pepper.

Serves 8   SARA CUTTING

FISH EN PAPILLOT

4 fresh filets (sole, halibut, snapper,
   etc.) same size, approximately ½
   lb. each
½ cup mayonnaise or salad dressing
salt and pepper
2 tomatoes sliced thin
1 small onion, sliced very thin
1 green pepper, seeded and sliced
   thin
2 T. sherry or white wine (optional)

Spread each filet with mayonnaise or salad dressing. Salt and pepper to taste. Lay one fish filet on a double layer of foil (or single layer of heavy duty foil) twice the size of fish. Top with tomato slices, then onion slices, then green pepper slices. Sprinkle with wine if desired. Top with second filet, mayonnaise side down. Fold foil around the fish, leaving some room. The foil should be sealed tightly. Repeat with remaining 2 filets. Place on covered grill for 20 minutes. Open foil and serve (must be eaten immediately). Can also be done with any size filets. They should be paired by size. Cooking time must be adjusted..

Serves 4   SALLY DeROULET

TOMATOES STUFFED WITH VERMICELLI

8 tomatoes
Pesto Sauce:
   ½ cup fresh basil leaves, washed/
     dried
   1½ cloves garlic
   ¼ cup grated Parmesan cheese
   ¼ cup grated Romano cheese
   2 T. olive oil
½ lb. vermicelli, cooked
2 oz. pine nuts
salt and pepper to taste
grated Parmesan cheese
fresh basil leaves for garnish

Hollow out tomatoes and remove seeds. Drain tomatoes upside down. Blend all Pesto Sauce ingredients in blender until smooth. (Makes about ½ cup sauce.) Place cooked vermicelli (hot or cold) in large bowl. Toss with Pesto Sauce and pine nuts. Season with salt, pepper and grated Parmesan to taste. Fill tomatoes with pasta; top with basil leaves and serve. One-half pound vermicelli fills 8 tomatoes.

Serves 8   BRENDA K. ASHLEY

ORANGES FILLED WITH FRUITS

6 large navel oranges
4 stiffly beaten egg whites
sugar
1 qt. strawberries or raspberries
1/3 cup orange juice
1/3 cup Grand Marnier
1 tsp. grated orange rind
3/4 cup orange marmalade
juice of 1 lemon
1/2 tsp. ground ginger
pomegranate seeds or fresh
    currants

Cut oranges in half; remove pulp. Brush egg whites on the halves; roll in sugar. Place berries in the shells. Chill. Blend remaining ingredients except seeds. Chill. Pour over berries in shells just before serving. Decorate with seeds.

Serves 12   MRS. R. HENRY NORWEB, JR.

CHOCOLATE MACAROONS

2 oz. unsweetened chocolate
1-14 oz. can sweetened condensed
    milk
2 cups finely shredded coconut
1 cup chopped nuts
1 T. strong brewed coffee
1 tsp. almond extract
1/8 tsp. salt

Combine chocolate and milk. Cook over medium heat, whisking, until thick and glossy. Remove from heat, add other ingredients. Drop mixture by small teaspoonsful on a greased baking sheet. Bake at 350 degrees 10 minutes.

Yield: about 5 dozen   MRS. R. HENRY NORWEB, JR.

"EL SALON MEXICO"

Sangria
*Mexican Popover Casserole
Salad with Tarragon Salad Dressing
*Pineapple Walnut Cake

MEXICAN POPOVER CASSEROLE

1 lb. ground beef
2-8 oz. jars taco sauce
¼ cup chopped green pepper
¼ cup chopped onions
2 T. cornmeal
½ tsp. salt
½ tsp. pepper
1 tsp. parsley flakes
1-12 to 15 oz. can corn
2 cups shredded cheddar cheese
2 eggs
1 cup milk
1 cup flour
1 T. oil
½ tsp. salt
2 T. chopped green onions or black
  olives (optional)

Preheat oven to 425 degrees. In large skillet, brown then drain ground beef. Stir in taco sauce, green pepper, onions, cornmeal, ½ tsp. salt, pepper and parsley. Heat to boiling and stir 1 minute. Pour into ungreased 9 x 13-inch pan. Sprinkle corn on top, then cheese over corn. Beat eggs, milk, oil, flour and ½ tsp. salt together, then pour over cheese. Sprinkle with onions or olives, if desired. Bake at 425 degrees for 25 to 30 minutes until golden and puffy. Serve immediately.

Serves 6 to 8   SALLY DeROULET

PINEAPPLE WALNUT CAKE

2 eggs
2 cups cake flour
2 cups sugar
2 tsp. baking soda
1 tsp. vanilla
½ cup chopped walnuts
1-15½ oz. can crushed pineapple
and juice

Combine all ingredients in a large bowl. Mix with a spoon until well blended. Pour into an ungreased 9 x 13-inch pan. Bake at 350 degrees for 35 to 40 minutes. Cool cake, then frost. Refrigerate before serving.

FROSTING

8 oz. cream cheese, softened
½ cup butter
1½ cups powdered sugar
1 tsp. vanilla

Cream cream cheese and butter. Add powdered sugar and vanilla and mix 2 minutes until smooth.

Serves 18 to 24   RUTH CRUSE

"COFFEE CANTATA"

Hot Spiced Tea
Coffee
*Pecan Rolls
*Strawberry Bread
*Pumpkin Muffins
Fresh Fruit

PECAN ROLLS

1 cake yeast
1¼ cups milk
½ cup sugar
½ lb. butter
2 eggs
4½ cups flour
½ tsp. salt
chopped pecans, raisins
¼ cup light Karo syrup
½ cup brown sugar
4 T. butter

Crumble yeast in ¼ cup warm milk. Melt butter in 1 cup warm milk and cool. Add sugar and eggs. Add yeast mixture to flour and salt. Combine both mixtures and mix thoroughly. Knead, refrigerate a few hours or overnight. Let warm to room temperature, roll into rectangle, spread with melted butter and sprinkle with sugar, cinnamon, chopped pecans and raisins. Roll up as jelly roll, slice in 1½-inch slices. Heat syrup, brown sugar and butter. Pour into buttered muffin tins. Sprinkle with chopped pecans. Put rolls on top and let rise until doubled in bulk; then bake 30 minutes at 350 degrees. Immediately turn on to wax paper, quickly scrape any sauce left in tins onto rolls.

Yield: 12 rolls   SALLY ROSENFIELD

STRAWBERRY BREAD

1-10 oz. box frozen strawberries
1½ cups flour
1 cup sugar
1½ tsp. cinnamon
½ tsp. salt
½ tsp. baking soda
2 eggs, beaten
½ cup oil

Thaw berries and drain. Reserve liquid. Mix together flour, sugar, cinnamon, salt and soda. Beat eggs, oil and berries. Slowly add dry ingredients. Pour into greased and floured 9 x 5-inch loaf pan. Bake at 350 degrees for 50 to 60 minutes. Strawberry butter: Mix reserved juice with one stick softened butter.

Serves 12   MARCIE AVILA

PUMPKIN MUFFINS

1½ cups flour
2 tsp. baking powder
¾ tsp. salt
½ cup sugar
½ tsp. cinnamon
½ tsp. nutmeg
4 T. butter
½ cup raisins
1 egg
½ cup cooked pumpkin
½ cup whole milk
1 to 2 T. sugar

Mix first 6 ingredients together. Cut in butter. Mix in raisins. In separate bowl, beat egg, then add pumpkin and milk. Add to butter mixture and mix only until blended. Fill greased muffin pans ⅔ full. Sprinkle ¼ tsp. sugar over each muffin. Bake at 400 degrees for 20 to 25 minutes.

Yield: 12 muffins   HELEN GREENLEAF

COUNTRY DINNER

*Pork Chops with Parmesan Cheese and
White Wine
New Potatoes
*Scalloped Carrots
*Thelma's Russian Tea Biscuits
California Zinfandel or Puligny Montrachet

PORK CHOPS WITH PARMESAN CHEESE AND WHITE WINE

6 pork chops, trimmed
salt and freshly ground pepper
**6 T. butter or margarine, room
temperature**
½ cup bread crumbs
½ cup grated Parmesan cheese
2 T. finely chopped shallots
¼ cup dry white wine

Season chops with salt and pepper. Melt 2 T. of butter or margarine in skillet. Add chops and cook until golden brown on both sides. Transfer to platter and keep warm. Blend bread crumbs, cheese and remaining 4 T. of butter or margarine. Divide mixture equally into 6 portions. Sprinkle shallots over bottom of skillet. Add wine and simmer for 1 minute, scraping particles from bottom of pan. Remove from heat. Arrange chops in shallow baking dish. Pat bread crumb mixture on each chop. Pour wine mixture around chops. Bake uncovered at 400 degrees 10 minutes. Cover loosely with foil and continue baking 20 minutes.

Serves 6   MARY ANNE SCHMITZ

SCALLOPED CARROTS

2 lbs. sliced, cooked carrots
¼ cup butter
¼ cup minced onion
¼ cup flour
2 cups milk
¼ tsp. dry mustard
¼ tsp. celery salt
2 cups (8 oz.) shredded cheese
1 cup buttered bread crumbs

Melt butter. Saute onion. Add flour. Add milk, stirring constantly. Add dry mustard, celery salt, and cheese. Stir. Add carrots. Place in buttered casserole. Top with buttered bread crumbs. Bake uncovered at 350 degrees for 25 minutes.

Serves 8 to 12   RUTH GRIFFIN

THELMA'S RUSSIAN TEA BISCUITS

4 cups flour
2 tsp. baking powder
1 stick butter
¾ cup sugar
½ cup oil
¼ cup orange juice
1 tsp. vanilla
3 eggs
8 oz. jar raspberry jam
½ cup yellow raisins
nuts
cinnamon mixed with sugar

Cream sugar and butter. Add flour, baking powder, oil, orange juice, vanilla and eggs. Roll between waxed paper to ¼-inch thick rectangle. Spread with jelly. Sprinkle with raisins, nuts, cinnamon sugar. Roll like jelly roll. Slice ¾-inch thick. Place on greased baking sheet. Brush with beaten egg. Sprinkle with sugar. Bake at 350 degrees for 30 minutes.

SALLY ROSENFIELD

AUTUMN COOKOUT

*Cider Sipper
*Hot Ryes
*Steve's Beach-Haven Chowder
BBQ Chicken
Corn on the Cob
*Cranberry Pudding Cake
or
*Pumpkin Mousse
California Zinfandel or Macon Lugny

CIDER SIPPER

½ gal. fresh apple cider, chilled
9 oz. vodka

Mix together and serve.

Serves 10   JENNY PERRY

HOT RYES

4 oz. grated Swiss cheese
¼ cup cooked crumbled bacon
½ cup chopped ripe olives
¼ cup chopped onion
1 tsp. Worcestershire sauce
¼ tsp. salt
¼ cup mayonnaise
1 loaf cocktail rye bread or a box of
   rye crackers

Mix all ingredients. Spread on bread, bake on ungreased cookie sheet for 10 minutes at 350 degrees.

CONNIE BUKVIC

STEVE'S BEACH-HAVEN CHOWDER

¼ lb. salt pork, diced
1 cup finely chopped onion
3 cups cold water
4 cups potatoes, diced
2 doz. fresh clams or 2-8 oz. cans of
    chopped clams
2 cups heavy cream
⅛ tsp. thyme
salt and pepper to taste
2 T. butter
paprika

In a soup pot, fry pork for 3 minutes over high heat. Reduce heat, add onions and cook 5 minutes. Add water and potatoes. Bring to a boil, then simmer half covered for 15 minutes. Add clams, cream and spices. Bring to a boil. Reduce heat and simmer until served.

Serves 6   NANCY GAGE

CRANBERRY PUDDING CAKE

2 cups flour
2 tsp. baking powder
½ tsp. salt
1 cup sugar
1 cup milk
3 T. melted butter
2 cups cranberries

Mix all ingredients. Pour into 8 x 8-inch greased pan. Bake 1 hour at 350 degrees. Top with Sauce.

SAUCE

¼ lb. butter
1 cup sugar
¾ cup cream

Mix ingredients for sauce. Bring to a boil. Serve hot over individual pieces of warm or cool cake.

Serves 9 to 12   MRS. E. R. O'DAY

PUMPKIN MOUSSE

1 cup pumpkin
½ tsp. cinnamon
½ tsp. ginger
½ tsp. nutmeg
¼ tsp. ground cloves
1-1 oz. envelope unflavored gelatin
¼ cup rum
¼ cup water
4 eggs
⅔ cup sugar
1 cup heavy cream, whipped
sweetened whipped cream

Combine pumpkin and spices. Stir gelatin, water and rum over low heat until dissolved. Beat eggs until light; add sugar and continue beating 10 minutes. Combine pumpkin, gelatin and egg mixtures. Fold in whipped cream. Pour into souffle dish or individual bowls. Refrigerate several hours. Serve with sweetened whipped cream.

Serves 8   LORI HANSON

"BOLERO"

*Snappy Shrimp Parmesan
*Tomato and Onion Pizza
Green Salad
*Cantaloupe Sorbet
*Hungarian Loveknots
Chablis Grand Cru or California Pinot Blanc

SNAPPY SHRIMP PARMESAN

1 lb. raw, peeled, deveined shrimp,
   fresh or frozen
1 tsp. chopped fresh chives
½ clove garlic, minced
¼ cup butter
1 tsp. salt
1½ T. sherry
1 T. grated Parmesan cheese

Thaw shrimp if frozen. In 10-inch frying pan, saute chives and garlic in butter until tender. Add shrimp and simmer 2 to 3 minutes or until largest shrimp is opaque in center when cut in half. Add sherry and sprinkle cheese over shrimp. Serve warm.

Serves 6   DIANE GILL

TOMATO AND ONION PIZZA

½ pkg. dry yeast or ½ cake yeast
1 cup lukewarm water
2½ cups flour
½ tsp. salt
2 T. olive oil

Dissolve yeast in water. Add 2 cups flour and salt to yeast. Stir in olive oil. Form dough and knead in remaining flour until smooth. Oil bowl, add dough, turning it to coat with oil; cover with damp cloth. Leave to rise in warm place 45 minutes or until doubled in bulk.

TOPPING

4 T. olive oil
6 large onions, thinly sliced
3 T. Dijon mustard or to taste
1 cup grated Parmesan cheese
6 tomatoes, cored and sliced
salt and pepper to taste
¼ cup freshly chopped basil and
    parsley, mixed

In large skillet cook onions in oil for 20 minutes. Punch down dough, divide in half. Roll each half on lightly floured board into a thin 12-inch round. Transfer to large buttered baking sheet. Spread each with ½ the mustard. Top with onions and parmesan cheese. Set tomatoes on onions in concentric circles. Sprinkle with salt and pepper. Pour some oil from cooking the onions on top. Bake pizzas at 475 degrees 20 to 25 minutes, until crust is golden and crisp. Sprinkle with parsley and basil mixture.

Serves 6 to 8   SHERYL JULIAN

CANTALOUPE SORBET

4 cups peeled, sliced cantaloupe
2 cups fresh orange juice
2 tsp. fresh lemon juice
1 cup sugar
1 cup marsala
2 egg whites
fresh mint leaves

Puree melon in blender or food processor until smooth. Pour into bowl and stir in orange juice, lemon juice, sugar and marsala. Cover bowl and freeze until mushy. In another bowl, beat egg whites until stiff. Remove partially frozen cantaloupe mixture from freezer and whip smooth. Fold egg whites into melon mixture. Cover and refreeze until firm. Garnish with fresh mint leaves.

Serves 6 to 8   JOYCE MONACHINO

HUNGARIAN LOVE KNOTS
(Csöröge)

1 cup sour cream
4 egg yolks
2 cups sifted flour
1 T. rum (optional)
shortening for frying

Add flour to egg yolks, sour cream and rum to make a soft dough. Knead until smooth. Roll out very thin. Cut into diamond shapes, then make slit in the center, approximately 1½-inches long. Pull one end through center slit. Fry in deep hot fat until light brown. Drain on paper towel. Dust with powdered sugar when cool.

IRENE M. WALSH

42

BLOSSOM PICNIC

Cold Barbequed Chicken with
*Sugarless Barbeque Sauce
*Macaroni Salad
*Mint Brownies
Vouvray or California Chenin Blanc

SUGARLESS BARBEQUE SAUCE

2 onions, sliced
¾ cup water
½ tsp. black pepper
1 tsp. paprika
2 T. Worcestershire sauce
1 tsp. chili powder
¾ cup catsup
2 T. vinegar
1 tsp. salt

Heat all together.

MRS. CHARLES HUSAK

MACARONI SALAD

1 lb. spiral macaroni
¼ cup milk
1 red onion, chopped
2 large tomatoes, chopped
2 small green peppers, chopped
½ cup sour cream
1½ cups mayonnaise
1 T. beef bouillon powder
2 tsp. red wine vinegar
1 tsp. dill

Cook macaroni and drain well, then toss with milk.
Add onion, tomato and green pepper. Toss remaining ingredients with macaroni mixture. Refrigerate.

Serves 10 to 12   LINDA KRESNYE

MINT BROWNIES

1 cup butter
1½ cups sugar
4 eggs
2 tsp. vanilla
1 cup sifted flour
¾ cup cocoa
1 tsp. salt
1 tsp. baking powder
¾ cup coarsely chopped nuts
Mint Frosting and Glaze

Cream butter and sugar until light and fluffy. Beat in eggs, one at a time. Add vanilla. Sift flour, cocoa, salt and baking powder together. Blend into butter mixture. Stir in nuts. Spread in greased 9 x 13-inch pan. Bake at 350 degrees for 20 to 30 minutes until edges are slightly firm and center still soft. Cool; frost with Mint Frosting then freeze 30 minutes. Then apply glaze and immediately cut into bars.

MINT FROSTING

2 cups sifted confectioners' sugar
¼ cup softened butter
2 T. milk
1½ tsp. mint extract
few drops green food color

Combine ingredients, beating thoroughly.

GLAZE

½ cup chocolate bits
1 T. butter
1½ T. water

Melt chocolate and butter. Add water, blend well.

Yield: 36 to 42 bars   LINDA KRESNYE

SUPER BOWL SUNDAY

*Zucchini Soup with Curry
*Handy-Dandy Sandwiches
Potato Sticks
*Orange-Buttermilk Cookies

ZUCCHINI SOUP WITH CURRY

**¼ cup butter
4 medium zucchini, sliced
2 small onions, chopped
2 cloves garlic, pressed
½ to ¾ tsp. curry powder
1 cup cream or milk
2-13 oz. cans chicken broth
½ tsp. salt
sour cream, parsley, chives or green
    onion for garnish**

In large skillet, melt butter. Add zucchini, onion, garlic and curry. Steam, covered, until tender, stirring occasionally. Put in blender and puree. Return to saucepan, or put in a casserole in which you can both cook and serve. Add cream or milk, and broth. Salt to taste. Heat and stir until well blended. Serve hot, or chill several hours or overnight. Garnish with sour cream and chives, parsley, or chopped green onions.

Serves 6 to 8   GINGER KUPER

HANDY-DANDY SANDWICHES

1½ lbs. sliced bacon
½ to ¾ cup chili sauce
4 to 6 T. sweet pickle relish
1-5 oz. jar dried beef, shredded
1 medium onion, minced
6 slices cheddar or American cheese
6 hard rolls or hamburger buns

Fry bacon until crisp; drain and crumble into a bowl. Add chili sauce, relish, shredded beef, and onion. Divide mixture onto 6 split rolls; sprinkle with cheese, then cover with tops. Wrap individually in foil. Bake at 300 degrees for 20 to 30 minutes.

Serves 6   HELEN GREENLEAF

ORANGE-BUTTERMILK COOKIES

¾ cup butter
1 cup sugar
1 egg
2½ cups flour
½ tsp. salt
½ tsp. baking soda
½ cup buttermilk
3 T. orange juice
2 tsp. grated orange rind

Cream butter and sugar. Beat in egg. Sift together flour, salt and soda. Add dry ingredients alternately with buttermilk. Stir in juice and rind. Drop by teaspoonfuls onto an ungreased cookie sheet. Bake at 375 degrees for 10 minutes. Cool.

ICING

1½ cups confectioners' sugar
3 T. orange juice
1 tsp. grated orange rind

Mix together. Spread on cooled cookies.

BARBARA LEUKART

Concertos

Festive Feasts

Pierce

MENU FOR ALL SEASONS

*Country Tomato Soup
*Veal Escallopes Marsala
Broad Noodles
*Green Salad with French Dressing
*Pecan Roll
Nebbiola D'Alba or Vouvray

COUNTRY TOMATO SOUP

½ cup butter or margarine
1 small clove garlic minced
1 cup chopped celery
1 cup chopped onion
½ cup chopped carrots
½ cup chopped zucchini
¼ cup flour
2-1 lb. 12 oz. cans whole tomatoes
2 T. brown sugar
1 tsp. marjoram
1 bay leaf
4 cups chicken broth
2 cups half & half
½ tsp. paprika
½ tsp. curry powder
¼ tsp. white pepper
salt to taste

Saute garlic, celery, onion, carrots, zucchini in butter until tender. Stir in flour. Cook 2 minutes stirring constantly. Add tomatoes, brown sugar, basil, marjoram, bay leaf, chicken broth. Cover. Simmer 30 minutes. Discard bay leaf. Puree mixture in food processor or blender. Add half & half, paprika, curry powder, white pepper. Stir. Add salt. Garnish with sunflower seeds, if desired. Serve hot or cold.

Yield: 12 cups   MARCIA BALL

VEAL ESCALLOPES MARSALA

1 lb. veal escallopes
flour well-seasoned with salt and
   pepper
6 T. butter
1 T. olive oil
⅔ cup Marsala

Cut veal in very thin slices and pound paper thin.
Coat with flour. In large pan, heat butter and oil.
Add veal and brown on both sides. Add Marsala and
simmer, covered, for 10 minutes.

Serves 4   VIRGINIA WALTER

FRENCH DRESSING

1 cup olive oil
¾ cup sugar
¾ cup ketchup
2 cups cider vinegar
½ tsp. salt
½ small onion, minced

Mix above ingredients and blend well. Store in
refrigerator. Shake well before using. Serve at room
temperature.

Yield: 1 quart   ANITA SMITH

PECAN ROLL

4 eggs, separated
1 cup sifted confectioners' sugar
2 cups ground pecans
1 cup whipping cream
3 T. sugar
2 tsp. cocoa
½ tsp. vanilla

Preheat oven to 400 degrees. Grease a 10 x 15-inch pan and line with waxed paper then grease paper. Beat egg yolks and sugar until thick and lemon-colored. Beat whites until stiff but not dry. Fold yolks and nuts into whites. Blend gently, but thoroughly. Spread evenly into pan. Place in oven and reduce heat to 350 degrees. Bake 15 to 20 minutes until springy. Remove from pan right side up. Roll cake from short end without removing wax paper. Cool rolled up. Whip cream with sugar, cocoa and vanilla until soft peaks form. Unroll cake, remove wax paper, and spread with whipped cream. Reroll cake. Dust top with confectioners' sugar and refrigerate.

Serves 8 to 10   NANCY L. WALSH

"SEA SYMPHONY"

*Sole with Almonds
Rice
Honey Glazed Carrots
Salad
*Fluden
Pouilly Fuissé or White Graves

SOLE WITH ALMONDS

⅓ cup flour
1¼ tsp. salt
¼ tsp. freshly ground pepper
1½ lbs. sole filets
6 T. butter
1 T. oil
2 T. lemon juice
½ cup sliced almonds
2 T. butter

Preheat oven to 225 degrees. Saute almonds in 2 T. butter until golden. Remove from pan and set aside. Combine flour, salt and pepper. Coat each filet. In a large skillet, heat 3 T. butter and oil. Pan fry filets over medium heat until golden, about 1 to 2 minutes on each side. Do not crowd in pan. Transfer to oven-proof platter and place in oven. Fry remaining filets, adding more butter as needed. When done, turn heat to high, add lemon juice to pan and cook for a few seconds. Pour lemon butter over fish and garnish with almonds.

Serves 4   CHERYL LEWIS

FLUDEN
(LAYERED APPLE RAISIN CAKE)

3 eggs
¾ cup sugar
¾ cup melted shortening
3 cups of flour (more if needed)
juice of 1 orange
juice of ½ lemon
pinch of salt
1 tsp. vanilla
2 heaping tsp. of baking powder
½ tsp. baking soda
chopped nuts
cinnamon sugar
coconut
plum jelly
sliced apples
raisins

Beat eggs with sugar. Add lemon and orange juice; then shortening, vanilla and salt. Mix slightly and set aside. Combine baking powder, soda and flour. Add flour mixture to egg mixture and knead into dough. (Add more flour if dough is sticky.) Refrigerate for 30 minutes then divide dough into 4 pieces. Roll out 1 piece and place in a greased and floured 9 x 13-inch baking pan. Spread plum jelly over dough. Arrange apple slices on top, then sprinkle with raisins, coconut, cinnamon sugar, and chopped nuts. Continue rolling out dough and layering in same manner. End with dough on top. Sprinkle with cinnamon sugar and nuts. Bake at 400 degrees for 10 minutes. Then lower oven to 350 degrees and bake about 50 minutes longer or until golden brown on top and done in center. Cut into small squares while warm.

Serves 12   DEBORAH WEISS

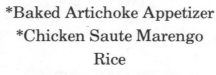

"THE GOLDEN COCKEREL"

*Baked Artichoke Appetizer
*Chicken Saute Marengo
Rice
*Mom's Nut Torte
Côte Rotie or Petite Syrah

BAKED ARTICHOKE APPETIZER

**1 can artichokes, drained
1 cup mayonnaise
1 cup grated mozzarella cheese
1 cup grated Parmesan cheese**

Mix ingredients. Spoon into 1-quart baking dish. Bake at 350 degrees for 30 minutes. Serve hot with crackers.

THE COMMITTEE

CHICKEN SAUTE MARENGO

**4 chicken joints
¼ cup butter
6 small peeled onions
2 tsp. paprika
3 T. tomato puree
10 oz. beer
1 bay leaf
5 oz. light cream
seasoning to taste**

Brown chicken in butter. Add onions and cook until onions soften. Season and add paprika. Stir in tomato puree and beer. Add bay leaf. Cover and simmer until chicken is tender (about 45 minutes). Remove bay leaf. Skim fat and stir in cream. Simmer until heated through.

Serves 4

MRS. JEAN HODGEKINS

MOM'S NUT TORTE

12 eggs separated
1½ cups sugar
1½ cups ground walnuts
4 whole graham crackers, ground
grated rind of ½ lemon
1 tsp. rum or whiskey
1 tsp. vanilla
1 tsp. cinnamon
1 tsp. lemon juice
1 recipe Custard Frosting

Beat egg yolks and sugar until lemony. Fold in vanilla, rum, cinnamon, lemon rind, and juice. Fold in nuts and graham cracker mixture. Gently fold in egg whites beaten stiff but not dry. Pour into three greased and floured 9-inch layer pans. Bake at 375 degrees for 10 minutes, reduce heat to 325 degrees for 15 minutes. Frost when cool.

CUSTARD FROSTING

1 egg
½ cup sugar
2 heaping T. flour
1 cup milk
1 T. instant coffee (optional)
1 tsp. vanilla
1 cup butter

Cream eggs and sugar. Add flour and milk and beat until smooth. Add coffee. Cook over low heat, stirring constantly until comes to a boil. Remove from heat. Add vanilla. Refrigerate until cold. Beat butter into cold custard about 10 to 15 minutes.

Serves 12 to 16   LINDA KRESNYE

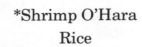

"LA MER"

*Shrimp O'Hara
Rice
Sauted Zucchini with Tomatoes
*Minetry's Miracle
Muscadet or California Chardonnay

SHRIMP O'HARA

4 T. butter
½ cup celery, chopped
½ cup green pepper, finely chopped
1½ lb. raw shrimp
½ tsp. curry
½ tsp. dill weed
2 cups (or less to taste) sour cream
salt to taste

Peel and devein raw shrimp. Cut shrimp lengthwise if desired. Saute celery and green pepper in butter until soft. Add shrimp and saute until cooked. Sprinkle salt, dill weed and curry over shrimp and vegetables. Add 2 cups sour cream (or less) and stir until heated through.

Serves 6   RUTH GRIFFIN

MINETRY'S MIRACLE

1 lb. sweet butter
2 cups sugar
1 dozen eggs, separated
1 lb. Amaretti (Italian macaroons)
1 cup Bourbon
4-1 oz. squares unsweetened choco-
    late (melted and cooled)
1 tsp. vanilla
1 cup chopped pecans
2 dozen ladyfingers
1½ cups heavy cream, whipped for
    decoration

Cream butter and sugar together until light and fluffy. Beat yolks until light then beat into creamed mixture. Soak macaroons in Bourbon (macaroons should be fresh from bakery — not prepackaged "hard" cookie type). Beat melted chocolate into butter mixture. Add vanilla and pecans. Beat whites until stiff but not dry. Fold into chocolate mixture. Line a 10-inch springform pan (on bottom and sides) with split ladyfingers. Alternate layers of macaroons and chocolate in pan. Chill overnight. Remove sides and decorate if desired with whipped cream.

Serves 16 to 20   BRENDA K. ASHLEY

"ROMAN CARNIVAL OVERTURE"

*Italian Sausage Hunter's Style
*Neapolitan Salad
Pasta
Toasted Garlic Bread
*J.B.'s Lemon Souffle
Barbera or Chianti Classico

ITALIAN SAUSAGE HUNTER'S STYLE

**4 lbs. fresh sausage, cut in 6-inch
   pieces (sweet or hot, or a mixture)
8 T. oil
4 cloves garlic, chopped
2 onions, sliced
4 green peppers, sliced
16 large mushrooms, quartered
4 oz. brandy
8 oz. red wine
4 T. tomato paste
2 cups stock, chicken or beef
4 bay leaves
pinch of basil
salt and pepper**

Place the sausage in a pot with the oil. Cover and cook over medium heat for 5 minutes. Occasionally uncover to turn the sausage, or shake the pot to prevent sticking. Add the garlic, onion, green pepper and mushrooms, and saute for another 5 minutes. Add the remaining ingredients and simmer, partially covered, for about 10 minutes stirring occasionally.

Serves 8   JENNIFER LANGSTON

NEAPOLITAN SALAD

2 large cauliflower florets
1 tsp. salt
½ tsp. pepper
4 T. wine vinegar
10 T. olive oil
2 T. capers
2 tsp. minced parsley
2 doz. pitted, chopped black olives
sweet red pimento

Cook florets in boiling water for 7 minutes. Drain, chill. Mix remaining ingredients. Combine with florets. Garnish with red pimento.

Serves 8   GINNA HERMANN

J.B.'S LEMON SOUFFLE

1-1 oz. envelope unflavored gelatin
½ cup cold water
⅛ tsp. salt
4 egg yolks
1-6 oz. can lemonade (frozen)
grated rind of one lemon
4 egg whites
½ cup sugar
½ pint whipping cream, whipped

Soften gelatin in cold water in saucepan. Add salt, egg yolks, beat thoroughly. Cook, stirring constantly until gelatin dissolves. Beat in lemonade and rind. Chill, stirring, until mixture mounds when dropped from a spoon. Beat egg whites, gradually adding sugar until stiff peaks form. Fold into gelatin mixture. Fold in whipping cream. Turn into 1-quart souffle dish or into individual dessert dishes. Chill until firm.

Serves 6 to 8   JOYCE BRAUN

PATIO LUNCH

*Banana-Orange Slush
*Eggs Madras
*Raisin Bran Muffins
*Cold Raspberry Souffle
Grey Reisling

BANANA-ORANGE SLUSH

- 1 cup sugar
- 2 cups boiling water
- 1-6 oz. can orange juice concentrate, undiluted
- 1-15¼ oz. can crushed pineapple, undrained
- 3 bananas, peeled and sliced
- 2½ T. lemon juice
- 1-10 oz. jars maraschino cherries, drained
- mint sprigs for garnish (optional)

Combine all ingredients in bowl. Mix well. Cover. Refrigerate for 24 hours stirring occasionally. Freeze overnight or until firm. Remove from freezer 15 to 20 minutes before serving to allow fruit to "slush." Makes a delicious addition to brunch, lunch or dinner. Can be kept frozen for a month or more.

Yield: 2 qts. or 10 to 12 servings   MRS. L.A. BURNS

EGGS MADRAS

6 hard cooked eggs
½ cup chutney, chopped
salt
½ cup mayonnaise
1 to 2 T. curry powder
1 tsp. soy sauce
milk or cream

Slice eggs in half lengthwise. Mash yolks and mix with chutney. Fill whites with yolk mixture. Combine mayonnaise, curry powder, soy sauce. Add milk or cream to desired consistency. Spoon this sauce over the eggs. Serve on bed of lettuce for first course, or with thick curry sauce as a finger appetizer (messy).

Serves 4   MRS. ROBERT NEARY

RAISIN BRAN MUFFINS

1-15 oz. box Raisin Bran cereal
2½ cups sugar
5 cups flour
5 tsp. soda
2 tsp. salt
1 cup melted shortening or oil
4 beaten eggs
1 qt. buttermilk

Mix cereal, sugar, flour, soda, and salt. Add remaining ingredients and mix well (by hand). Pour into greased muffin tins. May store in refrigerator up to 5 or 6 weeks. Bake at 375 degrees for 20 minutes.

Yield: 5½ dozen   LOIS McCORMICK

COLD RASPBERRY SOUFFLE

1-10 oz. pkg. frozen raspberries
1-1 oz. envelope gelatin
4 eggs, separated
½ cup sugar
pinch of salt
¼ cup sugar
1 cup heavy cream, whipped to hold
  peak

Oil a 1-quart souffle dish. Use a 6-inch piece of wax paper and make a 3-to-4-inch collar around the dish. Thaw the raspberries and drain well. Sprinkle the gelatin over ¼ cup raspberry juice to soften. Puree raspberries and remaining juice. Set aside. In a double boiler, beat egg yolks slightly and gradually beat in ½ cup sugar and pinch of salt. Cook mixture over simmering water, stirring constantly until thickened (may take 5 to 7 minutes). Remove and stir in gelatin until dissolved. Let mixture stand until cool but not set. Beat egg whites until they hold a shape and gradually beat in ¼ cup sugar to make a shiny meringue. Beat heavy cream, until thick, not stiff. Fold egg whites into berry mixture. Fold whipped cream into berry puree. Combine both mixtures. Pour into prepared dish and chill 2 to 3 hours then remove collar.

Serves 4 to 6   SUSAN LEVINE

Variation:

1 lb. fresh raspberries
¼ cup cold water

Reserve 8 raspberries for decoration. Puree and sieve the remainder. Follow above directions using water to soften gelatin. Decorate when set with raspberries and pistachio nuts.

THE COMMITTEE

HEARTY FARE

*Company Pork Chops
*Squash Casserole
Buttered Peas
Tossed Green Salad
Rolls
*French Silk Pie
California Johannisberg Reisling

COMPANY PORK CHOPS

6 to 8 pork chops
2 to 4 slices pineapple cut in half
1 thin slice lemon per chop
1 slice onion (thin) per chop
1 T. brown sugar per chop
1 T. chili sauce per chop

Place chops in baking dish. On each chop place ingredients above in stated order. Cover and bake at 350 degrees for 30 minutes. Uncover, bake 30 to 45 minutes until browned, basting frequently.

Serves 6 to 8   MRS. JOHN LADD DEAN

SQUASH CASSEROLE

4 large yellow squash
½ stick butter
3 eggs
2 T. sugar
¼ cup all-purpose flour
1 T. baking powder
salt and pepper to taste

Cook squash. Scoop out pulp, mash. Add butter and remaining ingredients. Pour into greased casserole. Bake in 325 degree oven for 1 hour.

Serves 6 to 8   MRS. BORIS CHUSID

FRENCH SILK PIE

Crust:
- 3 egg whites
- ¼ tsp. cream of tartar
- ⅛ tsp. salt
- ¾ cup sugar
- ½ cup ground pecans

Filling:
- ½ cup butter
- ¾ cup sugar
- 1 square unsweetened chocolate, melted
- 1 tsp. vanilla
- 2 eggs

Crust: beat egg whites until frothy. Add salt and cream of tartar. When soft peaks form, slowly add sugar. Beat until very stiff. Fold in pecans. Place in well-greased 9-inch glass pie pan. Bake at 275 degrees 1 hour or until dry. Filling: cream together butter and sugar. Add cooled chocolate and vanilla. Add eggs, one at a time, beating 5 minutes after each addition. Pour filling into crust and chill at least 1 hour. Serve with additional whipped cream.

Serves 6 to 8   DIANNE VOGT

LIGHT 'N EASY

Cold Plum Soup
*Chicken and Watercress Sandwiches
*Crab in a Pocket
Assorted Relishes
*Emily's Southern Pound Cake
Vouvray or California Chenin Blanc

CHICKEN AND WATERCRESS SANDWICHES

**1 loaf homemade white bread
1 stick butter, softened
1 T. curry powder
watercress
mayonnaise
chicken breast, cooked, skinned
and sliced thin**

Freeze loaf of bread for 2 hours. Cut off crusts and slice into ¼-inch slices. Mix softened butter and curry powder. Spread one side of each slice with curry butter. Top with watercress sprigs. Spread sprigs lightly with mayonnaise. Arrange sliced chicken breast over them. Spread chicken lightly with mayonnaise. Top with watercress sprigs, then top with bread, buttered side down. Stack sandwiches, wrap in a dampened tea towel and chill. Cut sandwiches into 1½-inch thick slices.

Serves 12   BARBARA BOHLMAN

CRAB IN A POCKET

1½ lb. crabmeat
1¼ cups mayonnaise
3 green onions, chopped
1 T. seasoning salt
1½ tsp. lemon juice
2 tomatoes, chopped
8 to 10 oz. shredded mozzarella or
    provolone cheese
6 small-size pita breads, cut in half

Combine all ingredients, fill all 12 pockets with filling. Lay on baking sheet and bake at 350 degrees until pita bread is lightly crisped (15 to 20 minutes). Makes 12 half sandwiches.

SHIRLEY SCHOENBERGER

EMILY'S SOUTHERN POUND CAKE

½ lb. butter, softened
3 cups sugar
3 cups flour
6 eggs at room temperature
1 T. vanilla
1 T. almond flavoring
chopped almonds (optional)
½ pint heavy cream

Cream butter and sugar. Beat in eggs one at a time. Add flavorings and almonds. Alternately add cream and flour. Butter and flour loaf pan. Bake for 1 hour and 15 minutes at 325 degrees. Start with cold oven.

Serves 12

DENISE CRENSHAW

"EVENING SONGS"

Shrimp Cocktail

*Chicken in White Wine

Rice Pilaf

*Broccoli and Cheese Puff

*Mandarin Cocoa Torte

Graves Sec or Piesporter Goldtropfchen

CHICKEN IN WHITE WINE

2 whole chicken breasts
salt
nutmeg
2 T. butter
2 T. onion, minced
¼ lb. mushrooms, sliced
⅔ cup dry white wine
1 tsp. cornstarch
2 tsp. additional wine

Bone, skin, halve breasts. Sprinkle with salt and nutmeg. Brown in butter. Add onion, mushrooms and wine. Bring to a boil. Cover, reduce heat, simmer 15 minutes. Remove chicken to warm platter. Bring pan juices to a boil, stirring until reduced slightly. Mix cornstarch with 2 teaspoons of wine, stir into juices until thickened. Spoon sauce over chicken.

Serves 4   MARCIA BALL

BROCCOLI AND CHEESE PUFF

3-10 oz. pkgs. frozen, chopped
   broccoli
½ cup margarine
pinch of pepper
16 oz. jar processed cheese spread
2 cups crushed Ritz Crackers

Cook broccoli. Drain. Mix with remaining ingredients. Spoon into 1½-quart buttered casserole, bake 30 minutes, at 350 degrees.

Serves 6   SUE SZABO

MANDARIN COCOA TORTE

Cheese custard:
  8 oz. cream cheese
  ½ cup sugar
  3 eggs
Cocoa:
  ½ cup butter
  1 cup sugar
  ⅓ cup cocoa
  1 tsp. vanilla
  2 eggs
  ½ cup flour
  ½ cup chopped nuts
Glaze:
  2 T. cornstarch
  1½ T. sugar
  1 cup orange juice
  1 small can mandarin oranges

Beat cream cheese until smooth. Gradually add ½ cup sugar and continue beating at medium speed 2 minutes. Add 3 room-temperature eggs, 1 at a time. Beat 5 minutes until light and fluffy. Cream butter and 1 cup sugar. Add cocoa and vanilla. Cream 3 minutes. Add 2 eggs, 1 at a time, beat 1 minute. Remove from mixer. Add flour, chopped nuts, and stir until mixed. Grease bottom only of two 8-inch cake pans. Put wax paper on bottom then turn greased side up. Divide cocoa mix evenly between pans. Pour cheese evenly on top of cocoa in each pan. Bake 30 minutes at 350 degrees. Let stand 10 minutes. For the glaze, mix cornstarch and sugar. Gradually stir in juice. Bring to boil over medium heat, stirring constantly. Simmer 2 to 3 minutes. Remove one cake from pan. Remove paper. Turn cheese side up on serving plate. Spread glaze over layer. Put other layer on top. Spread glaze over tops and sides. Decorate with oranges. Let stand 30 minutes at room temperature, then refrigerate until served.

Serves 10 to 12   NANCY L. WALSH

"LE MIDI"

*Sallie's Pasta Potpourri
*Herb Bread
*Pears in Wine
*Chocolate Chews
Frascati

SALLIE'S PASTA POTPOURRI

12 oz. bulk Italian sausage
1 cup sliced fresh mushrooms
2 tsp. dried basil, crushed
½ tsp. salt
¼ tsp. garlic powder
2 eggs
¼ cup milk
½ cup grated Parmesan cheese
8 oz. spaghetti noodles
¼ cup butter
12 cherry tomatoes, halved

In a 10-inch skillet brown sausage; add mushrooms. Cook until mushrooms are tender; drain. Stir in basil, salt and garlic powder; keep warm. In mixing bowl, beat eggs slightly; stir in milk and cheese. Set aside. Meanwhile, in large saucepan cook spaghetti according to package directions; drain. Return to saucepan, add butter, stirring until melted and well combined. Add meat mixture and egg mixture; blend well. Stir in tomatoes. Turn into serving dish. Serve immediately.

Serves 4 to 6   VICKIE FRANKENBURG

HERB BREAD

2 cups warm water (105-115 degrees)
2 pkg. active dry yeast
2 T. sugar
2 tsp. salt
2 T. soft butter
½ cup + 1 T. Parmesan cheese
1½ T. dried oregano leaves
4½ cups sifted all-purpose flour

Sprinkle yeast over water in large bowl. Let stand for a few minutes; stir to dissolve. Add sugar, salt, butter, ½ cup cheese, oregano, 3 cups flour. Beat on low speed until blended. At medium speed beat until smooth, 2 minutes. Scrape bowl and beaters with wooden spoon. Gradually beat in remainder of flour. Cover bowl with waxed paper and towel. Let rise in warm place free from drafts for 45 minutes or until lightly bubbly and more than double. Preheat oven to 375 degrees. Lightly grease 1½ or 2-quart casserole, or 2 loaf pans. With wooden spoon stir down batter. Beat vigorously ½ minute or 25 strokes. Turn into greased casserole or pans. Sprinkle evenly with Parmesan cheese. Bake 55 minutes, until brown. Turn out onto wire rack.

SALLY SYME

PEARS IN WINE

2½ lbs. fresh pears
2 cups dry white wine
½ cup sugar
1 lemon
1-2 inch length cinnamon, or ¼ tsp.
  ground
1 tsp. vanilla extract
¼ cup orange marmalade
¼ cup apricot preserves

Peel and core the pears and cut them into eighths. Place in a saucepan and add wine and sugar. Peel the lemon and cut the peel into fine julienne strips (make sure you have no pith). Add the peel to saucepan. Bring to a boil and simmer 5 to 10 minutes or until pears are tender. Transfer pears and lemon to serving dish. Bring liquid to a boil again and add remaining ingredients. Bring to a boil again and cook 10 minutes. Pour sauce over pears. Chill before serving.

Serves 6 to 8   NANCY L. WALSH

CHOCOLATE CHEWS

½ cup vegetable oil
4 squares unsweetened chocolate,
   melted and cooled
2 cups sugar
4 eggs
2 tsp. vanilla
2 cups flour
2 tsp. baking powder
½ tsp. salt
confectioners' sugar

Mix oil, chocolate and sugar. Blend in eggs one at a time. Add vanilla. Stir flour, baking powder, and salt into oil mixture. Chill 2 to 3 hours, or overnight. Roll about one teaspoon of dough into ball, then roll in powdered sugar. Place on greased cookie sheet 2 inches apart. Bake 10 to 12 minutes at 350 degrees. Nuts and dates can be added to dough if desired.

Yield: 3 to 4 dozen   DIANE GILL

"LES NUITS D'ÉTÉ"

*Crab Rice Squares
Grilled Steaks
*"Pasta House" Salad
Browned Potatoes
*Lemon Meringue Pie
Cahors or California Chardonnay

CRAB RICE SQUARES

3 cups long-grain rice, cooked
2 cups milk
1 cup grated cheddar cheese
1-6 oz. can crabmeat, drained
3 eggs, beaten
¼ cup minced parsley
¼ cup minced onion
¼ cup minced pimiento
1 tsp. Worcestershire sauce
Curry Shrimp sauce

Preheat oven to 325 degrees. Grease a 9 x 13-inch baking dish. Combine first 9 ingredients and blend thoroughly. Pour into dish. Bake 45 minutes until set. Cut into squares. Spoon sauce over each serving.

CURRY SHRIMP SAUCE

1 can cream of shrimp soup
½ cup sour cream
1 tsp. lemon juice
½ tsp curry powder

Combine all ingredients in top of double boiler set over simmering water and cook, stirring constantly, until heated.

Serves 12   DIANE GARDNER

"PASTA HOUSE" SALAD

1 head iceberg lettuce
⅓ head romaine lettuce
1-4 oz. jar pimiento
1-8 oz. jar artichoke hearts, drained
1 large red onion, sliced
½ cup Parmesan cheese
salt and pepper, to taste
⅓ cup red wine vinegar
½ cup olive oil

Combine first 7 ingredients. Combine vinegar and oil and shake well. Pour over lettuce mixture. Toss and marinate in refrigerator 1 hour.

Serves 6   RUTH CRUSE

LEMON MERINGUE PIE

1 9-inch pie shell, baked
1½ cups boiling water, divided
1¼ cups sugar
5 T. cornstarch
2 eggs, separated
⅛ tsp. salt
2 large lemons, juice, grated rind
2 tsp. sugar
½ tsp. cream of tartar

Boil 1¼ cups water and sugar together until sugar dissolves. Add cornstarch moistened with ¼ cup of water. Cook three minutes until clear. Remove from heat. Add egg yolks, salt, lemon juice, rind. Cook for two minutes. Cool slightly. Turn into pie shell. Beat egg whites with sugar and cream of tartar until shiny. Spread over pie filling. Brown under broiler for a few minutes.

Serves 8   IRENE M. WALSH

SPRING DINNER

*Chilled Strawberry Soup
*Lamb Wassail
Parslied New Potatoes
*Baked Celery
*Grandma Sharkey's Cheesecake
Gigondas or California Merlot

CHILLED STRAWBERRY SOUP

1½ cups water
¾ cup dry rosé wine
½ cup sugar
2 T. fresh lemon juice
1 2-inch cinnamon stick
1 qt. strawberries (pureed)
½ cup whipping cream
¼ cup sour cream

Combine water, wine, sugar, lemon juice, and cinnamon. Boil uncovered 15 minutes. Add strawberry puree and boil 10 minutes more, stirring occasionally. Discard cinnamon and chill. Whip cream. Combine with sour cream. Fold into strawberry mixture. Serve chilled. Garnish with mint leaves and a dollop of sour cream.

Serves 6   MEREDITH BASS

LAMB WASSAIL

1 frozen leg of New Zealand spring
   lamb (5 or 6 lbs. defrosted)
1 cup Burgundy or dry red wine
¼ cup water
1 clove minced garlic
2 T. grated onion
zest of one lemon, cut in thin strips
½ tsp. salt
½ tsp. cinnamon
¼ tsp. nutmeg

Bone and trim excess fat from lamb with sharp knife. Cut slits in meat. Combine all seasonings. Pour over meat and marinate 1½ to 2 days. Turn occasionally. Drain lamb, reserve marinade. Place lamb, fat side up, on rack in appropriate pan; brush with reserved marinade. Roast at 325 degrees for about 1 hour and 45 minutes or until meat thermometer reads 140 degrees. Allow to rest 10 minutes before slicing.

Serves 6 to 8   DIANE GILL

BAKED CELERY

4 cups celery, sliced diagonally
1-3 oz. can sliced water chestnuts
1 can cream of mushroom soup
¼ cup diced pimiento
¼ cup soft bread crumbs, buttered
¼ cup sliced almonds

Cook celery in salted water 8 minutes; drain. Mix remaining ingredients (except crumbs) with celery. Place in casserole. Sprinkle on buttered crumbs. Bake at 350 degrees for 35 minutes.

Serves 6 to 8   MRS. ALFRED J. HART

GRANDMA SHARKEY'S CHEESECAKE

2-8 oz. pkg. cream cheese
1 lb. small curd cottage cheese (well drained)
1½ cups sugar
4 eggs
1 stick (¼ lb.) butter
1 T. lemon juice
⅓ cup cornstarch
1 pint sour cream
¾ cup graham cracker crumbs

Cream the cream cheese. Add cottage cheese. Beat well. Add sugar. Beat in eggs one at a time. Add cornstarch, lemon juice and butter. Add sour cream last. Grease a 10-inch spring-form pan. Sprinkle with graham cracker crumbs. Pour cheese mixture over crumbs. Bake at 325 degrees for 1 hour until cake comes away from sides of pan. Allow cake to cool in oven after it is turned off.

Serves 12   KATHY ROCKMAN

"ROYAL FIREWORKS MUSIC"

*Oriental Salmon Barbeque
*Rice Salad
*Chocolate Chocolate Chip Cake
California Pinot Noir or
California Sauvignon Blanc

ORIENTAL SALMON BARBEQUE

1½ lbs. salmon steaks or filets
½ cup sweet wine or sherry
2 tsp. honey
2 tsp. prepared horseradish
¼ cup soy sauce
½ tsp. pepper
4 scallions, coarsely chopped
2 T. sesame or peanut oil

Combine wine, honey, horseradish, soy sauce, pepper and scallions. Place in shallow dish, add salmon and marinate, refrigerated, for 2 to 3 hours turning once. Coat grill with oil; have coals grey-hot. Place fish on grill. Add 2 T. oil to marinade. Brush fish with marinade as it cooks, approximately 7 minutes on first side and 5 minutes on second side, or until fish flakes.

Serves 4

MARTHA AARONS
THE CLEVELAND ORCHESTRA

RICE SALAD

2½ cups long-grain white rice
3 tomatoes, cored
1-10 oz. pkg. frozen peas
2 stalks celery
2 yellow squash
2 green peppers
1 red pepper
5 carrots
½ cup white wine vinegar
1 tsp. Dijon mustard
salt and pepper to taste
1½ cups oil

Bring a large pan of water with a slice of lemon to boil. Add 1 tsp. salt and rice. Stir until rice returns to boil. Let rice bubble steadily, stirring occasionally, for 12 minutes exactly. Drain, set aside. Peel, seed and core tomatoes. Cut in strips. Put in a bowl. Pour boiling water over peas, let set for 1 minute. Drain, rinse with cold water. Add to tomatoes. Halve celery stalks lengthwise, cut thin slices on an extreme diagonal. Add to other vegetables. Cut a thick lengthwise slice from each side of squash. Discard remaining column of seeds. Halve the strips lengthwise, then slice very thinly on extreme diagonal. Add to other vegetables. Core and seed green and red peppers. Cut in ½-inch dice. Add to other vegetables. Trim and peel carrots and cut into ½-inch dice. Put carrots into a saucepan, bring to a boil, simmer 2 minutes, drain and rinse with cold water. Add to other vegetables. Refrigerate vegetables until just before serving. Prepare dressing by whisking vinegar, mustard, salt and pepper together. Add oil, a little at a time, whisking constantly. Pile the rice into a bowl, add dressing, correct seasonings, refrigerate. Stir in vegetables just before serving.

Serves 10   SHERYL JULIAN

CHOCOLATE CHOCOLATE CHIP CAKE

⅓ cup shortening
1 cup sugar
½ tsp. vanilla
2-2 oz. squares unsweetened choco-
    late, melted and cooled
1 egg
1¼ cups sifted all-purpose flour
½ tsp. soda
½ tsp. salt
¾ cup water
1½ cup semisweet chocolate pieces
1 cup chopped walnuts (optional)

Cream shortening and sugar until light and fluffy. Blend in vanilla and cooled chocolate. Add egg, beating well. Sift together flour, soda, and salt. Add to creamed mixture alternately with ¾ cup water beginning and ending with dry ingredients. Fold in 1 cup chocolate pieces and chopped walnuts. Spread batter in greased and lightly floured 9 x 9-inch pan. Sprinkle with remaining chocolate pieces. Bake at 350 degrees for 45 minutes or until cake tests done. Dust with confectioners' sugar when cooled.

Serves 8   KATIE LORETTA

"SORCERER'S APPRENTICE"

*Veal Blanket
Buttered Noodles
Tossed Salad
*Apple Tart
Chateau Leoville Las Cases
California Cabernet

VEAL BLANKET

1 onion chopped
½ lb. veal stew in chunks
¼ tsp. basil
freshly ground pepper
¼ cup white wine
½ cup chicken broth
**½ lb. mushrooms, halved and
sauteed**
**1-10 oz. package frozen artichoke
hearts**
2 tsp. cornstarch

Brown onion in 10-inch frying pan using 2 tsp. cooking oil. Remove onion from pan. Brown veal on all sides using high heat. Add oil if necessary. Add onion, wine, basil and pepper. Cover and bake at 260 degrees for 1 to 2 hours until tender. Add chicken broth only as needed to moisten pan. When meat is tender, add remaining broth and enough water to make one cup. Stir in cornstarch and thicken over low heat. Add sauteed mushrooms and defrosted artichokes and heat through.

Serves 3 to 4   DOTTIE SCHNELL

APPLE TART

1½ cups flour
1 cup ground almonds
¼ cup sugar
1 egg, beaten
½ cup butter
3 cups pared, cored and sliced
  apples
1 T. lemon juice
2 T. flour
¼ tsp. ground cinnamon
¾ cup orange marmalade, divided
2 T. butter
¼ tsp. almond extract

Prepare pastry: combine flour, almonds and sugar. Cut in butter until mixture resembles coarse crumbs. Stir in egg. Mix first with fork, then with fingers until dough holds together. Reserve ½ cup dough for lattice; press remainder into bottom and sides of 9-inch fluted flan pan. Refrigerate until ready to fill. Prepare filling: toss apples with lemon juice. Combine apples with 2 T. flour, cinnamon and ½ cup orange marmalade. Place in pastry-lined pan; dot with butter. Roll remaining pastry in a 9-inch round; cut into ¾-inch strips. Weave a lattice over apples; trim edges even with pan. Bake at 325 degrees for 40 minutes or until apples are tender. Cool 15 minutes. Melt remaining ¼ cup marmalade; stir in almond extract. Spoon over filling between lattice strips.

Serves 8   VICKIE FRANKENBURG

Symphonies

Glorious Galas

Pierce

"SYMPHONIE FANTASTIQUE"

*Scaloppine Cleviden
*Fettucine
Tomatoes Provencal
Pear Sorbet
*Easy Chocolate Truffles
Brunello Di Montalcino or Corvo

SCALOPPINE CLEVIDEN

**10 thin slices veal (scaloppine),
about 1½ lbs.
salt and freshly ground pepper to
taste
flour for dredging
1 egg
2 cups seasoned bread crumbs
3 T. olive oil
3 T. butter
juice of ½ lemon
6 thin, seeded lemon slices
fresh parsley for garnish**

Pound veal until very thin. Trim veal of fat and cut into 2 x 4-inch slices. Sprinkle with salt and pepper and dredge lightly in flour. Beat egg, dip veal in egg, then in bread crumbs. Heat 1½ T. oil and 1½ T. butter in a skillet and cook the veal, 3 or 4 pieces at a time, until golden brown on both sides. Remove veal and place on paper towels. Add remaining oil and butter and continue cooking the rest of the veal. Add more oil and butter if needed. Place veal in baking dish, cover and bake in 350 degree oven for 15 minutes. Uncover and cook for 5 minutes. Squeeze juice of ½ lemon over meat. Garnish with lemon slices and parsley.

Serves 4   DONNA CATLIOTA

FETTUCINE

¼ cup margarine
4 eggs
¼ cup heavy cream
8 oz. bacon, cooked
1 lb. fettucine
1 cup Parmesan cheese
pepper to taste
¼ cup chopped parsley

Two-and-one-half hours before serving time, take out eggs, cream and margarine and allow them to come to room temperature. Cook fettucine in boiling salted water for about 15 minutes. Meanwhile beat together eggs and cream just until blended. Heat oven-proof serving dish in 250 degree oven. Drain fettucine thoroughly, but DO NOT RINSE. Turn pasta into heated dish. Toss pasta with margarine. Pour egg mixture over pasta and toss until pasta is well coated. (Heat from pasta cooks eggs and thickens sauce.) Add bacon, cheese, pepper and parsley; toss to mix. Serve immediately.

Serves 6   MARY ANN GREINER

EASY CHOCOLATE TRUFFLES

8 oz. unsweetened chocolate, grated
2 sticks sweet butter
¾ lb. confectioners' sugar
1 T. Grand Marnier
4 oz. sweetened chocolate, grated

Put unsweetened chocolate, butter, confectioners' sugar and Grand Marnier into food processor. Blend until smooth. Take 1 teaspoon of chocolate mixture and roll into a tiny ball in the palm of your hand. Roll the truffle in the sweet, grated chocolate. Put truffles on lined serving plate or into candy cups.

Yield: 40 to 50   SUSAN LEVINE

"THE CREATION"

*Baked Sole with Raspberry Sauce
*Richard Nelson's Spoonbread Souffle
*Auntie's Favorite Nut Cake
California Chardonnay

BAKED SOLE WITH RASPBERRY SAUCE

6-6 oz. filets of sole (or salmon or halibut)
½ cup white wine
¼ cup clarified butter
salt to taste
white pepper to taste
2 sliced lemons
1 cup red wine vinegar
2 T. red raspberry puree
2 T. sugar
1 cup cream
dash salt
½ tsp. lemon juice
1 tsp. chopped shallots
½ cup butter

Brush baking dish with clarified butter. Skin filets, season, and place skinned side down in dish. Sprinkle with white wine and lay lemon slices on top of fish. Cover with foil and bake at 350 degrees for 20 minutes or until fish flakes easily. Prepare sauce: bring vinegar, puree, sugar, cream, salt, lemon juice and shallots to boil. Reduce heat and simmer until liquid is reduced to about ⅔ cup or until mixture is syrupy. Remove from heat and whisk in 2 T. butter at a time. (Hold at room temperature.) Transfer fish to serving platter. Pour sauce around fish and serve.

Serves 6   BONNIE FEMEC

RICHARD NELSON'S SPOONBREAD SOUFFLE

2 cups cold milk
½ cup white cornmeal
½ cup butter
1-6 or 7 oz. roll garlic pasteurized
    processed cheese
4 eggs, separated
1 tsp. baking powder
1 tsp. sugar
½ tsp. salt

Mix cold milk and cornmeal in a 2-quart saucepan. Cook over medium heat, stirring occasionally, until consistency of thick cream sauce. (Be careful not to burn.) Remove from heat. Stir in butter until melted. Add cheese. Stir until smooth. Cool. Add well-beaten egg yolks, baking powder, sugar and salt. Beat egg whites until stiff but not dry. Fold into cornmeal mixture. Pour into well-buttered 2-quart souffle dish. Bake at 350 degrees for 45 to 50 minutes, until top is puffed and golden.

Serves 6   MRS. WILLIAM J. WILLIAMS

AUNTIE'S FAVORITE NUT CAKE

Bottom layer:
  1 cup + 2 T. flour
  15 T. butter
  1 to 2 T. sour cream
  ¼ cup sugar
  2 egg yolks
Filling:
  6 oz. apricot jam
Top layer:
  7 T. sugar
  3 eggs
  2 egg whites
  1 cup walnuts ground very fine
  2 T. lemon juice
  rind of ½ lemon
  powdered sugar

Lightly butter a 9 x 13-inch pan. Cut butter into flour with pastry blender until well blended. Add sour cream, sugar and egg yolks. Mix until blended. Spread in pan. Spread jam over dough. In mixer combine sugar, eggs, egg whites and mix for 5 minutes. Add nuts, lemon juice and rind. Pour filling over jam. Bake at 350 degrees for 35 to 40 minutes. Cool slightly. Cut in 1½-inch squares. Sprinkle with powdered sugar.

Yield: 40 squares   CYNTHIA CARR

HOLIDAY DINNER

*Roast Duck
Wild Rice
Parkerhouse Rolls
Creamed Peas
*Cranberry Conserve
*Ranch Pudding with Whipped Cream
Fleurie or German Rhinekabinet

ROAST DUCK

5½ lbs. duck, quartered
juice of one lemon
2 tsp. salt
1 tsp. juniper berries (crushed)
pinch crumbled sage
1 T. butter
1 medium onion, chopped
6 ribs celery (including tops)
1½ cups heated sherry
6 oz. fresh mushrooms

Trim excess fat from duck and prick skin to allow fat to drain while roasting. Rinse and dry. Place duck in large bowl. Pour lemon juice over pieces, turning once. Let stand 30 minutes. Remove from bowl. Rub pieces with salt, juniper berries and sage. Place skin side up on rack. Dot with butter. Roast at 450 degrees for 20 minutes. Turn and cook 10 minutes more. Drain off all fat and turn over. Reduce heat to 350 degrees. Add onion and celery to pan. Roast 2 more hours, basting every half hour. Cover pan for last hour of cooking. Add mushrooms 30 minutes before serving.

Serves 4   NANCY L. WALSH

CRANBERRY CONSERVE

1 lb. fresh cranberries
2 cups sugar
¾ cup chopped walnuts
1-12 oz. jar orange marmalade
2 T. lemon juice

Mix cranberries, sugar and walnuts in large pan and cover with foil. Center in 350 degree oven and bake for 30 minutes. Remove and stir well. Return to oven for 30 minutes more. Remove and add marmalade and lemon juice. Stir well and chill. Will keep refrigerated up to 2 months.

Yield: 4 cups   JOAN GRETTER

RANCH PUDDING WITH WHIPPED CREAM

1 cup dark brown sugar
¾ cup light corn syrup
4 eggs
¼ cup whiskey, rum, or brandy
¼ cup butter or margarine
1 tsp. vanilla
½ tsp. salt
1 cup chopped walnuts or pecans
1 cup raisins
½ cup walnut or pecan halves
whipped cream

Butter a 9 x 9-inch baking dish. Sprinkle 1 cup nuts and raisins evenly on bottom. Combine brown sugar, corn syrup, eggs, whiskey, melted butter, vanilla and salt in bowl and blend well. Pour over nuts and raisins. Arrange nut halves on top. Bake at 400 degrees for 10 minutes. Reduce temperature to 325 degrees and bake 25 minutes more. Serve warm with whipped cream.

Serves 6   MEREDITH BASS

"MOLL ROE"

*Gaelic Steak
Mashed Potatoes with Minced Parsley
*Vegetable Crunch Salad
*Double Chocolate Threat
French Bordeaux Rouge
California Cabernet Sauvignon

GAELIC STEAK

beef filets (one per person)
2 T. butter or margarine
1 onion, sliced
½ lb. fresh mushrooms, sliced
½ cup Irish Whiskey
½ cup heavy cream
salt and pepper

Melt butter or margarine in frying pan. Brown beef filets on both sides; remove from pan and set aside. In same pan, cook onion and mushrooms. When cooked, remove from pan and set aside. Add Irish Whiskey; stir in pan, picking up accumulated juices; add heavy cream. Return filets, onion and mushrooms to pan; add salt and pepper. When filets are cooked to degree you like, serve.

Serves 4   VINCENT DOWLING

VEGETABLE CRUNCH SALAD

2 cups broccoli florets
2 cups cauliflower florets
1 cup sliced celery
1 cup cherry tomatoes (whole)
1 cup sliced zucchini
¾ cup sliced green onion
½ cup pitted ripe olives, sliced
½ cup sliced carrots
1 cup (8 oz.) Italian Dressing (oil-
free dressing can be used)
Bacon bits (optional)
Shredded cheddar cheese
(optional)

In large bowl, combine all ingredients except bacon and cheese. Cover well and marinate in refrigerator 4 hours or overnight. Stir occasionally. Just before serving toss with bacon and cheese.

Serves 8   SANDY ABOOKIRE

DOUBLE CHOCOLATE THREAT

⅓ cup butter
2 squares unsweetened chocolate
1 cup sugar
2 eggs, well beaten
⅔ cup flour
½ tsp. baking powder
¼ tsp. salt
1 tsp. vanilla
1 cup whipping cream, for garnish

Melt butter and chocolate in top of double boiler over hot water. Remove from heat; add sugar and eggs, mix well. Sift together flour, baking powder and salt. Stir into chocolate. Add vanilla. Pour into greased and floured 8 or 9 inch square baking pans. Bake at 350 degrees for 20 minutes. Cool. Remove brownie from pan and cut into strips wide enough to fit the sides of a 2-quart spring form pan. Cut strip in half to make 2 thinner layers. Line the bottom and sides of pan with the brownie layers. Spoon prepared filling into brownie-lined pan, wrap well and chill overnight. To serve, loosen from sides of pan with knife, then dip into hot water. Unmold onto serving plate. Whip cream until stiff and cover top and sides of cake.

FILLING

1½ lbs. semisweet chocolate
½ cup strong coffee
3 eggs, separated
½ cup coffee liqueur
½ cup whipping cream

Melt chocolate with coffee in top of double boiler over hot water. Remove from heat. Beat yolks well. Stir into chocolate. Add liqueur. Cool. Beat egg whites until stiff but not dry. Whip cream until stiff. Fold whites and cream into chocolate mixture.

Serves 12   LYNNE ALFRED

"OISEAUX EXOTIQUES"

*Tom's Pheasants
Wild Rice
Green Salad Vinaigrette
*Chocolate Decadence
Le Corton or Puligny-Montrachet

TOM'S PHEASANTS

2 pheasants
½ cup flour
½ cup olive oil
½ cup butter
1 clove garlic, split
¼ tsp. basil
2 shallots, minced fine
1 cup button mushrooms
1 large tomato, skinned and sliced
1 cup dry white wine
1 cup red wine
1 cup sour cream
salt and pepper

Quarter pheasants. Pour flour, salt and pepper in a paper bag and shake until mixed. Drop in pheasants, one piece at a time, shake to coat and set aside. In a large skillet heat oil and butter. Add garlic, remove when well browned. Add pheasants and brown well; remove and drain. Put 4 T. of olive oil-butter from pan into an earthenware casserole. Arrange pheasant sections in casserole. Sprinkle with basil; add shallots, mushrooms, tomato, salt and pepper. Pour wine over all. Cover and bake at 325 degrees for 1½ hours. Remove cover and continue baking 20 minutes more. Add sour cream, cover and bake 5 minutes.

Serves 4   THOMAS GRETTER

CHOCOLATE DECADENCE

1¼ lb. dark sweet chocolate
½ cup plus 2 T. (1¼ sticks) unsalted
butter
5 eggs
1 T. sugar
1 T. flour

1¼ cups whipping cream
2 T. powdered sugar
2 T. orange liqueur
1-10 oz. package frozen raspberries,
thawed

Prepare one day in advance. Preheat oven to 425 degrees. Melt 1 lb. chocolate with butter in double boiler; set aside. In large metal bowl over boiling water, beat sugar and eggs with wire wisk until sugar dissolves and mixture is warm. With electric mixer, immediately beat mixture until triple in volume (5 to 10 minutes). Fold flour and chocolate mixture into egg mixture. Pour into 8-inch round cake pan lined with parchment paper. Bake exactly 15 minutes, allow to cool. Place in freezer for at least 24 hours. When ready to serve, remove cake from pan and peel off paper. Place on serving plate. Whip cream with powdered sugar and orange liqueur until peaks form. Top cake with whipped cream mixture, reserving some for piping through pastry bag to make rosette decorations around top. With potato peeler, form curls from remaining chocolate and pile curls in center of whipped cream topping. Puree raspberries in blender and sieve out seeds. Allow cake to sit at room temperature for 30 minutes before serving. Serve with raspberry puree.

Serves 12   EVIE DOBRIN
                                  DOBIE'S CORNER

"EINE KLEIN NACHTMUSIK"

*Cream of Broccoli Soup
*Pork and Sauerkraut
Baked Potatoes
Hearty Rye Bread
*Chocolate Almond Cheesecake
Gewurztraminer or Gigondas

CREAM OF BROCCOLI SOUP

1 bunch broccoli
4 T. butter
6 T. flour
5 cups chicken stock
salt
freshly ground pepper
½ cup heavy cream
½ cup milk
¼ tsp. nutmeg
dash cayenne (optional)

Reserve enough broccoli florets for garnish. Cut remaining broccoli into 2-inch pieces. Place all but garnish into saucepan, add water to cover. Salt to taste. Cook about 5 minutes or until tender crisp. Cook garnish in separate pan. Immediately refresh the garnish, set aside. Drain the other broccoli and refresh. In large saucepan, melt butter. Add flour, whisking until flour bubbles up. Add chicken stock; stir until it comes to a boil and is thick and smooth. Add broccoli, not garnish, simmer uncovered about 30 minutes. Puree in processor or blender. Return to saucepan, bring to boil. Add salt and pepper to taste. Add cream, milk, nutmeg, pinch of cayenne and cooked garnish. Heat. Serve immediately.

Serves 6 to 8   KATHY FLEEGLER

PORK AND SAUERKRAUT

4 to 6 lbs. loin pork roast
2-16 oz. cans Bavarian-style
    sauerkraut
2 apples, cubed
1 large onion, sliced
4 T. brown sugar
1½ tsp. salt

Drain sauerkraut and put sauerkraut directly into shallow 10 x 12-inch roasting pan. Mix apples, onion, brown sugar and salt. Pour on top of sauerkraut. Salt meat and place on bed of sauerkraut. Roast at 350 degrees, 45 minutes per pound of meat. As meat juices seep into sauerkraut, move it around and from under meat so all sauerkraut gets flavor of meat and browns equally.

Serves 6   LYDIA HERFORTH

CHOCOLATE ALMOND CHEESECAKE

Crumb crust:
 1½ cups chocolate wafer crumbs
 1 cup blanched almonds, chopped
 ⅓ cup sugar
 6 T. butter, softened
Filling:
 1½ lbs. cream cheese, softened
 1 cup sugar
 4 eggs
 ⅓ cup heavy cream
 ¼ cup Amaretto or other almond-
  flavored liqueur
 1 tsp. vanilla
Topping:
 2 cups sour cream
 1 T. sugar
 1 tsp. vanilla
 slivered toasted almonds for
  garnish

Combine first 4 ingredients and press onto the bottom and sides of a buttered 9½-inch spring-form pan. Cream the cream cheese and sugar. Beat in eggs one at a time. Add heavy cream, liqueur, vanilla and beat until light. Pour into shell and bake at 375 degrees for 40 minutes. Cool on rack for 5 minutes. Combine topping ingredients, spread evenly over cake and bake for 5 more minutes. Transfer cake to a rack. Let it cool completely. Chill, lightly covered, overnight. Remove sides of pan and press almonds around the top edge.

Serves 8   BARBARA BOHLMAN

STRICTLY FOR COCKTAILS

*Marinated Shrimp
*Hot Cream Cheese Crab
*Chinese Barbequed Ribs
*Sauerkraut Balls
Assorted Crackers
*Mushroom Tartlets
*Herb Curry Dip
Assorted Vegetables
*Strawberry Meringue Tarts
*Chocolate Brandy Cheesecake

MARINATED SHRIMP APPETIZER

1 lb. fresh shrimp, shelled and deveined
celery tops
¼ cup pickling spice
2 cups sliced red onions
7 bay leaves
1½ cups salad oil
¾ cup white vinegar
3 T. capers and juice
2½ tsp. celery seed
½ tsp. salt
6 or 7 drops tabasco sauce

Bring water to boil, add pickling spices and celery tops and cook 5 minutes. Add cold, raw shrimp and simmer 3-5 minutes until cooked. Drain. In glass bowl, alternate shrimp, onions, and bay leaves. Mix together remaining ingredients and pour over shrimp mixture. Refrigerate at least 24 hours. Drain and serve with cocktail picks.

Serves 4 to 5   MRS. JOHN J. DWYER

HOT CREAM CHEESE CRAB

1-8 oz. pkg. cream cheese
1-3 oz. pkg. cream cheese
1 cup or more crab
3 T. chopped green onions and tops
1½ T. milk
1 tsp. horseradish
cracked pepper
sliced almonds

Cream together all ingredients except almonds. Put in shallow pie pan and bake at 375 degrees for 15 minutes or until bubbly. Garnish with sliced almonds. Serve hot or cold.

Serves 12 to 15   CAROLE KAY

CHINESE BARBEQUED RIBS

2½ to 3 lbs. baby-back pork ribs
⅔ cup brown sugar
6 T. crystallized ginger
¼ cup wine vinegar
1¼ cups water
⅔ cup soy sauce
2 cloves crushed garlic
2 T. cornstarch mixed with ¼ cup
    water

Arrange ribs on roasting rack with ¼ cup water on bottom of pan. Bake covered at 350 degrees for 1 hour 15 minutes. Combine remaining ingredients except cornstarch. Boil 1 minute, then thicken with cornstarch. Dip ribs in sauce and bake uncovered at 350 degrees for 45 minutes.

Serves 8 to 10   RUTH ANN BERGER

SAUERKRAUT BALLS

1 medium onion, minced
2 T. butter or margarine
1 cup finely minced ham
1 cup finely minced corned beef
½ tsp. garlic salt
1 T. prepared mustard
3 T. fresh parsley, minced
¼ tsp. black pepper
2 cups sauerkraut, drained and chopped
⅔ cup flour, divided
½ cup beef stock
2 eggs, well beaten
½ cup fine bread crumbs
½ cup cold mashed potatoes

Saute onion in butter until tender. Add ham, corned beef and cook, stirring often, for 5 minutes. Add garlic salt, mustard, parsley, pepper and sauerkraut. Mix. Add ½ cup flour and beef stock. Mix well. Cook for 10 minutes, stirring often. Spread mixture out on a platter to cool. When cool shape into 1-inch balls. Refrigerate for 1 hour. Roll each ball into remaining flour. Then, dip ball into beaten eggs and roll into bread crumbs. Deep fry until golden brown. Drain on paper towels.

Yield: 5 dozen   MRS. ROBERT WEAVER

MUSHROOM TARTLETS

1 stick butter
1 cup flour
1-3 oz. pkg. cream cheese
2 T. butter
½ lb. finely chopped mushrooms
2 T. finely chopped scallions
½ tsp. salt
½ tsp. pepper
1 T. flour
½ cup heavy cream

Prepare dough: in food processor, mix butter, flour and cream cheese until it forms a ball. Take walnut-size piece of dough and press into tart pan. Prepare filling: melt butter and saute finely chopped mushrooms, scallions, salt and pepper. Cook over medium heat until vegetables are soft. Sprinkle with flour and cook 1 minute. Add cream, cooking until thick. Put teaspoonful of mixture in each tart. Bake at 450 degrees for 10 minutes.

Yield: 24 to 30 small tarts   ·   DIANNE VOGT

HERB CURRY DIP

1 cup mayonnaise
½ cup sour cream
1 tsp. tarragon
¼ tsp. salt
⅛ tsp. curry powder
1 T. snipped parsley
1 T. grated onion
1½ tsp. lemon juice
½ tsp. Worcestershire
2 T. capers, drained

Blend all ingredients and chill well.

Yield: 2 cups   DIANNE VOGT

STRAWBERRY MERINGUE TARTS

3 egg whites at room temperature
½ tsp. almond extract
½ tsp. cream of tartar
dash of salt
1 cup sugar
1 cup sour cream
whole strawberries

Combine egg whites, almond extract, cream of tartar and salt; beat until frothy. Gradually add sugar, 1 T. at a time, beating until glossy and stiff peaks form. Do not underbeat. Drop meringue by tablespoonfuls onto cookie sheet that has been covered with heavy brown paper. Using back of small spoon, make a small depression in top of each meringue. Bake at 250 degrees about 30 minutes. Turn oven off and leave meringues in oven with door closed for 1 hour. Cool meringues away from drafts. Meringues may be stored in air-tight container. When ready to serve, place one tablespoon sour cream in each meringue; top each with a whole strawberry.

Yield: 25 to 40   MARGARET SIMON

CHOCOLATE BRANDY CHEESECAKE

1-8 oz. pkg. chocolate wafers
6 T. unsalted butter
3-8 oz. pkgs. cream cheese
1¼ cups sugar
5-1 oz. squares unsweetened baking
   chocolate
1-8 oz. carton sour cream
⅓ cup brandy
3 large eggs

Have eggs, cream cheese, and sour cream at room temperature when you start. Preheat oven to 350 degrees. Melt butter, and pulverize the wafers in a blender or food processor. Toss wafers with melted butter, mixing thoroughly; then sprinkle over bottom of a 10-inch spring-form pan and press down firmly. Melt chocolate in the top of a double boiler over barely simmering water. Thoroughly cream the cream cheese with the sugars, scraping bowl constantly. Beat in eggs one at a time; then the sour cream. Scrape the bowl once more. Mix in the melted chocolate and brandy. Pour into pan and place in oven. Immediately turn oven down to 275 degrees and bake for 1 hour and 15 minutes or until center is set and edges are puffy. Garnish with chocolate shavings when cool. Store in refrigerator. Serve at room temperature.

Serves 12   MARK KAPLAN

CELEBRATION DINNER

Champagne Punch
*Deviled Crab
Belgian Endive with Vinaigrette Dressing
*Beef Wellington
Green Beans Almondine
Assorted Rolls
*Normandy Chocolate Mousse
Pommard or Clos Vugeot

DEVILED CRAB

¾ cup milk
1 tsp. dry mustard
¼ tsp. paprika
½ tsp. salt
⅛ tsp. pepper
¾ cup bread crumbs
2 dashes tabasco sauce
3 hard-cooked eggs, diced
⅓ cup melted butter
½ tsp. Worcestershire sauce
2 T. mayonnaise
1½ cups flaked crab meat
3 T. sherry
Parmesan cheese

Mix all ingredients except Parmesan cheese. Put into shells and cover with extra buttered bread crumbs. Sprinkle with Parmesan cheese. Bake 20 minutes at 375 degrees. Fills 8 shells.

Serves 8   MARY NEWBOLD

BEEF WELLINGTON

1 filet of beef
¼ cup shortening
1 lb. mushrooms, finely chopped
1 T. chopped shallots
1 T. chopped onion
1 T. butter
½ tsp. salt
dash fresh ground pepper
1 T. chopped parsley
1 T. chopped chives
¼ cup heavy cream

Rich pastry:
2½ cups flour
1 tsp. salt
1 egg yolk plus milk to equal ½ cup
1 cup butter
1 egg white

Place filet and shortening in shallow pan. Roast in preheated 450 degree oven for 25 minutes. Cool. Saute shallots and onion in butter for about 1 minute. Stir in mushrooms and cook over low heat until liquid has disappeared and mushrooms are dark. Remove from heat. Season with salt, pepper, parsley and chives. Add cream and cool. To prepare pastry, cut butter into flour. Add salt, egg yolk, and milk. Roll pastry large enough to cover filet. Lift filet from pan and put a thick coating of mushroom mixture over entire surface. Wrap in pastry, brush with egg white, and bake in preheated 450 degree oven for 15 to 20 minutes or until golden brown. Meat will be rare. (Note: can be frozen before second baking. Remove from freezer 3 hours before brushing with egg white.)

Serves 8   RENA WIDZER

NORMANDY CHOCOLATE MOUSSE

1 lb. dark sweet German chocolate
2 oz. bitter chocolate
7 T. strong coffee
2 T. kirsch or rum
5 eggs, separated
4 T. sweet butter
1 cup heavy cream
2 dozen lady fingers

Put sweet and bitter chocolate and coffee in a heavy pan over low heat. Stir until the chocolate is dissolved, then add the kirsch or rum. Remove from heat. Add the egg yolks, one at a time, then add the butter bit by bit. Beat the cream over a bowl of ice until thick. Add slowly to the chocolate. Fold in the stiffly beaten egg whites. Lightly butter a 9-inch spring-form pan and line with split lady fingers. Fill with the mousse and chill overnight. Unmold before serving. Decorate with whipped cream and shredded chocolate if desired.

Serves 8   CHERYL LEWIS

"SONG OF THANKSGIVING"

*Cream of Chestnut Soup
Candied Cranberries
*Stuffed Cornish Game Hens
*Butternut Squash Casserole
Rolls
*Pumpkin Pie
California Sauvignon Blanc or Julienas

CREAM OF CHESTNUT SOUP

¼ **cup butter**
1 **medium onion, chopped**
3 **ribs celery, chopped**
2 **cups chicken broth**
1-1 **lb. jar peeled chestnuts, un-**
sweetened
2 **T. softened butter**
1 **T. flour**
1 **cup light cream**
salt or white pepper to taste

Melt butter in saucepan; add chopped onion and celery and cook until soft, but not brown. Puree mixture. Add the chestnuts and one cup of chicken broth and puree until smooth. Blend in remaining chicken broth. Return mixture to saucepan and bring to a boil. Knead 2 T. butter and the flour together until blended. Using a whisk, add a little at a time to hot soup mixture to thicken it. Season to taste with salt and pepper. Add cream and bring to a boil. If too thick, add more cream.

Serves 4   MRS. BEN M. HAUSERMAN

STUFFED CORNISH GAME HENS

4-1 lb. Cornish Game Hens, fresh or
thawed if frozen
2 small boxes wild rice mix
2 cups sliced mushrooms
6 stalks celery sliced
4 T. butter
1 to 1½ sticks butter

Rinse and drain hens. Sprinkle insides with salt and pepper and set aside. Cook wild rice according to instructions using slightly less water. (Can substitute white wine for half of water.) Set aside. Saute mushrooms and celery in 4 T. butter for 2 to 3 minutes. Combine rice, mushrooms and celery. Stuff hens with mixture. Melt butter and brush on outside of hens. Bake at 400 degrees for 10 minutes, then reduce heat to 350 degrees and continue baking an additional 40 to 50 minutes, basting with butter every 10 minutes or so.

Serves 4   SUZANNE MAXWELL

BUTTERNUT SQUASH CASSEROLE

2 cups fresh butternut squash,
peeled and cut into chunks
1 cup apples, peeled, cored and cut
into chunks
3 T. melted butter
3 T. brown sugar
1 tsp. nutmeg
¼ cup chopped pecans

Arrange squash and apples in layers in a 1½-quart casserole. Combine butter, brown sugar, nutmeg and pecans. Drizzle over all. Bake at 350 degrees for 1 hour.

Serves 4   SUZANNE R. BLASER

PUMPKIN PIE

1½ cups canned pumpkin
⅔ cup brown sugar
1 tsp. cinnamon
½ tsp. ginger
½ tsp. salt
2 eggs, slightly beaten
1½ cups milk
½ cup heavy cream
¼ tsp. cloves
allspice
1 9-inch unbaked pie shell

Mix all ingredients, except allspice together. Pour into unbaked pie shell. Sprinkle top with allspice. Bake at 450 degrees for 10 minutes; reduce heat to 350 degrees and continue baking 30 to 40 minutes longer.

Serves 8   TONY LOEHNERT

TREE TRIMMING PARTY

*Wassail
Eggnog
Salted Mixed Nuts
*See's Fudge
*Bourbon Balls
*Fruitcake Cookies
*Bavarian Cream Trifle
*Christmas Pudding

WASSAIL

**2 quarts apple cider or juice
½ cup brown sugar
1 tsp. whole allspice
1 tsp. whole cloves
3-in. stick cinnamon
1 cup brandy (optional)
orange slices**

Mix cider and sugar. Place spices in percolator basket or tie in cheesecloth. Perk or simmer 30 to 35 minutes. Remove spices. Add brandy and garnish with orange slices.

Serves 10   LINDA KRESNYE

SEE'S FUDGE

½ lb. butter or margarine
3 packages (6 oz.) chocolate chips
2 cups nuts
1 T. vanilla
4½ cups granulated sugar
1 tall can evaporated milk

In a large mixing bowl, mix the butter, chocolate chips, nuts and vanilla. In a large kettle, over low heat, stir the sugar and milk together until the sugar is dissolved. Increase heat slightly to bring to a rolling boil. Cook exactly 7½ minutes after reaching a rolling boil. Pour over contents of bowl. Stir until thoroughly mixed. Pour into a 13 x 9-inch pan. Let set and cut.

Yield: 4 pounds   MARY L. MOORE

BOURBON BALLS

2¼ cups finely crushed vanilla
    wafers
1 cup powdered sugar
2 T. cocoa
1 cup ground walnuts
3 T. light corn syrup
½ cup bourbon
½ to 1 cup powdered sugar (to roll
    balls in)

Mix wafers, 1 cup sugar, cocoa and nuts together. Add syrup and bourbon and mix. Roll in powdered sugar.

Yield: 3½ dozen   JENNY PERRY

FRUITCAKE COOKIES

1½ cups golden raisins
¼ cup diced citron
½ lb. chopped candied cherries
¼ cup rum
1 stick sweet butter
½ cup firmly packed brown sugar
2 eggs
1½ cups unsifted all-purpose flour
1 tsp. baking soda
2 tsp. ground cinnamon
½ tsp. ground cloves
½ tsp. ground nutmeg
⅛ tsp. salt
¼ lb. chopped pecans

Put raisins, citron and cherries in a bowl. Pour on rum or flavoring and let stand for at least one hour. Cream the butter. Add sugar and eggs and beat until fluffy. Sift flour with baking soda, spices and salt. Add to the butter mixture and blend well. Add nuts and the rum-soaked fruit. Cover and refrigerate overnight. Form batter into balls the size of walnuts. Bake on greased cookie sheets at 325 degrees for 10 to 12 minutes. Flavor improves on keeping.

Yield: 7 dozen   PATRICIA KORB

BAVARIAN CREAM TRIFLE

1 cup plus 2 T. white wine
3 envelopes unflavored gelatin
9 eggs, separated
1½ cups sugar
4½ cups milk
3 cups heavy cream
angel food or pound cake, sliced in
   slivers ½" thick
fresh or frozen unsweetened berries
   and peaches
sliced banana
red raspberry jelly

Pour wine into bowl and sprinkle with gelatin. Set five minutes. Heat slightly and stir until dissolved. Cool. Whisk egg yolks. Add sugar gradually and beat until thick. Beat in gelatin mixture. Stir in milk and transfer to heavy pan. Cook over high heat, stirring constantly until mixture coats back of metal spoon. (Do not overcook or mixture will curdle.) Mixture will be thin. Set over ice and whisk until cool. Beat egg whites until peaks form. Whip cream. Fold into egg yolk mixture. Spread cake slices with jelly and arrange on bottom and sides of trifle bowl. Spoon in portion of cream mixture. Add portion of fruits. Repeat cream, cake and fruits as desired ending with cream. Garnish with whipped cream or fruit slices. (Prepare one day in advance.)

Serves 16   HELEN REED

CHRISTMAS PUDDING

15 oz. raisins (dark)
15 oz. sultanas or light raisins
10 oz. currants
2 cups dark brown sugar
8 oz. mixed peel
8 oz. glacé cherries
grated rind of lemon
3 cups soft breadcrumbs
1 cup flour
4 oz. chopped almonds
2 cups finely chopped suet
1 tsp. salt
¼ tsp. nutmeg
6 eggs
½ pint brandy or rum

Mix dry ingredients in large bowl. Beat eggs and add with brandy or rum. STIR WELL. Put in 2 one-quart oven-proof bowls and cover with wax paper or foil and tie firmly leaving loops with which to lower pudding into saucepan of simmering water about one inch deep. Cook in simmering water for 3 to 4 hours. Be careful not to let the pan boil dry. This pudding keeps indefinitely in refrigerator and improves with age. Serve hot with Brandy Hard Sauce.

Serves 16   JEAN HOLDEN

ALSATIAN NEW YEAR'S DAY SUPPER

*Smoked Trout Paté
*Choucroute Garni
Boiled Potatoes
*Amaretto Chocolate Mousse
German Rhine Wine or Torres Coronas

SMOKED TROUT PATÉ

2 whole smoked trout
¾ cup unsalted butter, at room temperature
freshly ground black pepper, to taste
2 heaping tsp. drained green peppercorns
8 slices white bread, crusts removed
5 sprigs parsley (for garnish)

Pull skin from trout, removing spines and vertebrae. Separate the flesh from the bones and pick through the flesh to remove any small bones missed. Slice butter and work it with the smoked fish in a food processor or a little at a time in a blender until smooth. Pile into a bowl. Beat in the black pepper, green peppercorns, and pack the mixture into a 3-cup crock or divide it among 6 small ramekins. Smooth the tops and cover with plastic wrap. Refrigerate. Toast the bread and cut into triangles. Pile toasts around the molds and decorate the center(s) with parsley. Serve at once. (Also good served with melba toast.)

Serves 6   SHERYL JULIAN

CHOUCROUTE GARNI

2 T. oil
2 medium onions, sliced
1 clove garlic, minced
1 tart apple, pared and diced
1 carrot, sliced thin or grated
1 cup dry white wine or beer
1 bay leaf
8 juniper berries
10 peppercorns
2 cloves
parsley sprigs
2-16 oz. cans sauerkraut
1 lb. Canadian bacon, or ham, or
    smoked pork chops
4 knockwurst or other sausage

In a heavy pot or large skillet, cook the onions, garlic, apple, and carrot in oil until onion browns slightly. Add wine and herbs. Let simmer. Rinse sauerkraut until desired sourness is reached and press dry. Stir sauerkraut into pot, adding meats and cook until well heated, about 20 to 25 minutes.

Serves 4   MEREDITH BASS

AMARETTO CHOCOLATE MOUSSE

6 oz. pkg. semi-sweet chocolate
24 whole blanched almonds
½ cup Amaretto
2 envelopes unflavored gelatin
¼ cup water
4 egg yolks
⅓ cup sugar
2 cups milk
4 egg whites, beaten stiff
1 pt. whipping cream (not ultra-pasteurized)
2 pkgs. split lady fingers

Melt chocolate pieces over hot water. Dip bottom of each almond in melted chocolate and place on waxed paper. Chill almonds until chocolate is firm. To remaining melted chocolate, add Amaretto and stir well. Set aside. In saucepan, combine gelatin and water. Let gelatin soften. Then stir in egg yolks, sugar, and milk. Heat gently and stir until mixture thickens slightly and coats metal spoon. Stir in Amaretto-chocolate mixture. Chill until mixture mounds when spooned. Fold in beaten egg whites. Whip cream. Set aside 1 cup of whipped cream for trim (refrigerate). Fold in remaining whipped cream. Chill again until mixture mounds when spooned. Line bottom and sides of ungreased 9-inch spring-form pan with split lady fingers. Trim lady fingers so they don't extend above pan. Sprinkle with more Amaretto. Spoon partly-set chocolate mixture into lady finger "crust". Chill about 2 hours until firm. At serving time or an hour before, pipe 24 rosettes (using the reserved whipped cream) around edge of mousse. Press a chocolate-trimmed almond into center of each rosette so the chocolate part shows. Remove sides from spring-form pan and place dessert on serving plate.

Serves 10

CHERYL LEWIS

"A MIDSUMMER NIGHT'S DREAM"

*Paté Coquillette
*Spinach Stuffed Artichokes
*Filet a la Moutarde
Croissants
*Pears à l'Orange
Chambolle-Musigny or Savigny-Les-Beaune

PATÉ COQUILLETTE

½ lb. unsalted butter
¾ cup onions, chopped
1 small tart apple, peeled, cored and
    sliced
1 lb. chicken livers, cleaned, trimmed
1½ tsp. salt
freshly ground white pepper
¼ cup cognac
2 to 4 T. heavy cream
¼ lb. clarified butter

In heavy skillet, melt 3 T. butter. Add onions, cook until tender. Add apple, and cook 3 to 4 minutes longer. Transfer to blender or food processor. Add 3 T. butter to skillet and add chicken livers. Cook until brown (3 to 4 minutes). Season livers with salt and pepper, add cognac. Cook until cognac evaporates. Remove livers to chopping board and mince. Cool to room temperature. Add livers to apple mixture and add 2 T. cream. Blend until smooth. Cream 10 T. butter in bowl and add liver paste. Mix well. Pack mixture in small terrine and chill for 30 minutes or until very cold. Pour clarified butter on top, covering surface completely. Cover terrine with plastic wrap and chill 24 hours before serving. May be garnished with truffles.

Serves 8

KATHY COQUILLETTE

SPINACH STUFFED ARTICHOKES

1 lb. fresh spinach or 1-10 oz. pkg.
  frozen spinach
4 T. butter
salt to taste
dash nutmeg
pepper to taste
12 cooked artichoke bottoms
  (canned)
1½ cups thick Bechamel Sauce
6 T. grated Parmesan

Blanch spinach, drain and chop. Saute spinach in butter and add seasoning. Heap on artichoke bottoms. Top each with 2 T. Bechamel Sauce. Sprinkle with grated cheese. Brown in broiler.

BECHAMEL SAUCE

½ stick butter
1 cup flour
4 cups milk, heated
1 carrot, sliced
½ onion, stuck with cloves
Bouquet garni

Melt butter and stir in flour until smooth. Cook over low heat a few minutes and add milk. Stir until thickened. Add carrot, onion, and bouquet garni. Simmer 10 minutes and strain.

Serves 6   KATHERINE MAVEC

FILET A LA MOUTARDE

6 filet mignon steaks
3 T. butter
12 T. cream
6 T. cognac
3 T. Dijon mustard

Cook steaks in butter in a hot skillet to desired doneness. Remove steaks and keep warm. Rinse skillet with cognac; add cream, quickly stirring until sauce is reduced by half. Blend in mustard; pour over steaks.

Serves 6   CYNTHIA BAILEY

PEARS À L'ORANGE

6 ripe pears (preferably Bosc)
1 cup orange juice
grated peel of one orange
¼ cup Cointreau
juice of one lemon
3 to 4 T. honey
whipping cream

Cut the pears in half and core. Do not peel. Place pears cut side down in a shallow, buttered, oven-proof dish. Mix together the orange juice, grated rind, Cointreau, lemon juice and the honey. Pour over pears. Bake at 300 degrees for 20 minutes or until pears are tender. Baste often. Refrigerate pears in syrup until serving time. Serve very cold, with whipped cream (1 or 2 T.) and garnish with fresh mint if available.

Serves 6   DIANE GILL

String Quartets

Family Fare

Pierce

"THE SEASONS"

*Veal Meatballs
Rice
*Green Salad with Roquefort Dressing
*Hawaiian Pineapple Pound Cake
Schloss Volrades Spatlese

VEAL MEATBALLS

1 lb. ground veal
1 egg
¼ cup bread crumbs
1 small onion, grated
salt and pepper to taste
Sauce:
    1 large ripe tomato (2 medium)
    1 medium onion, cut into eighths
    1-8 oz. can tomato sauce
    salt and pepper to taste

Combine sauce ingredients in medium saucepan. Heat over low flame. Meanwhile, in a bowl mix veal, egg, onion and bread crumbs together. Shape into walnut size meatballs (about 12 to 14). Place meatballs in sauce, cover and cook 45 minutes.

Serves 4   SUSAN FLOWERMAN
THE CLEVELAND ORCHESTRA

ROQUEFORT DRESSING

½ lb. roquefort or blue cheese
1 cup "real" mayonnaise
1 cup sour cream

Crumble cheese with fork. Add mayonnaise and mix. Fold sour cream into mixture slowly. Do not beat.

DIANNE VOGT

125

HAWAIIAN PINEAPPLE POUND CAKE

1-20 oz. can crushed pineapple
¾ cup shortening
¾ cup butter or margarine
2½ cups sugar
5 large eggs
3 cups all-purpose flour
1 tsp. baking powder
¼ cup buttermilk
1 tsp. vanilla
1 T. rum, optional
glaze

Drain pineapple well; save syrup for glaze. Cream shortening, butter and sugar until light and fluffy. Add eggs, one at a time, beating well after each addition. Mix flour and baking powder. Set aside. Combine buttermilk, vanilla and rum. Add flour mixture to cake batter alternately with buttermilk mixture. Stir in crushed pineapple. Pour into a well-greased and floured large bundt pan or tube pan and bake at 325 degrees for 70 minutes or until cake tests done. Remove from oven and spoon half the glaze over cake. Let stand 10 to 15 minutes and then turn onto a serving plate. Spoon on remaining glaze. Cool before cutting.

GLAZE

¼ cup pineapple syrup
¼ cup butter or margarine
¾ cup powdered sugar
2 T. rum

Combine syrup, butter and sugar in a small sauce pan. Heat and stir until butter is dissolved and sugar is melted. Remove from heat and add rum.

REGINA DAILY

*Pork and Apple Casserole
Buttered Noodles
*Fudge Upside Down Cake
Gewurztraminer or Seyval Blanc

PORK AND APPLE CASSEROLE

2 lbs. fresh pork shoulder, cut into
  2-inch cubes
¼ cup flour
1½ tsp. salt
½ tsp. pepper
½ tsp. paprika
3 T. oil
1 large onion, sliced thin
1 bay leaf, crumbled
1 tsp. sage
1 clove garlic, chopped
1½ cups fresh cider, or
  1¼ cups cider, ¼ cup Calvados
4 carrots, sliced
2 tart apples, peeled, cored, sliced
1 cup celery, diagonally sliced
1 small turnip, in 2 x ½-inch sticks
chicken broth

Coat pork in flour mixed with 1 tsp. salt, ¼ tsp. pepper and paprika. Brown in heavy casserole. Remove and cook onion until golden. Return meat and add bay leaf, sage, garlic and cider. Bring to a boil, cover and bake at 350 degrees for one hour. Add carrots, apples, celery, turnips, ½ tsp. salt and ¼ tsp. pepper. Bring to a boil on top of stove and add chicken broth to barely cover vegetables. Cover and bake 30 minutes longer until vegetables are tender. Uncover last 10 minutes to thicken, if desired.

Serves 4 to 6   BARBARA LEUKART

FUDGE UPSIDE DOWN CAKE

1 T. shortening
¾ cup sugar
½ cup milk
1 tsp. vanilla
1 cup flour
1 tsp. baking powder
½ tsp. salt
1½ T. cocoa
¼ cup cocoa
½ cup white sugar
½ cup brown sugar
½ cup chopped nuts
1½ cups boiling water

Cream ¾ cup sugar and shortening. Add milk and vanilla. Sift flour, baking powder, salt and 1½ T. cocoa into mixture. Pour into a greased 8 x 8-inch cake pan. Prepare topping by combining ¼ cup cocoa, ½ cup white sugar and brown sugar. Spread nuts over batter, then cover with cocoa-sugar mixture. Pour boiling water over topping and batter. Bake at 350 degrees for 35 minutes. Cut into squares. Serve with whipped cream if desired.

Serves 8 to 10   MARCIA BALL

"COSI FAN TUTTE"

*5-Minute Crabmeat Spread
*Chestnut Chicken Casserole
*Four Minute Veggies
*Double Chocolate Pie
St. Veran

5-MINUTE CRABMEAT SPREAD

**1 pt. sour cream
6 oz. crabmeat (canned or frozen),
   drained
3 T. horseradish
1 pkg. Italian Dressing**

Mix all ingredients. Serve with party rye.

DOROTHY BERGOINE

CHESTNUT CHICKEN CASSEROLE

**2 cups cooked chicken
1 cup chopped celery
1 cup cooked rice
1 can cream of mushroom soup
1 small onion, chopped
¾ cup mayonnaise
1 can sliced water chestnuts
½ cup toasted slivered almonds
Topping #1:
   1 cup crushed cornflakes
   ½ stick melted butter
Topping #2:
   1 small bag potato chips, crushed
   ½ cup shredded cheddar cheese**

Mix ingredients; place in ungreased baking dish. Top with either topping. Bake at 350 degrees for 45 minutes.

Serves 4 to 6

MIMI CALFEE

FOUR MINUTE VEGGIES

**Leftover cooked or canned
   vegetables
Walnut or pecan pieces
Crumbled blue cheese**

Lightly grease a shallow pan or dish. Arrange vegetables in pan. Sprinkle with nuts, then blue cheese (sparingly). Broil three to five minutes.

BARBARA HAAS

DOUBLE CHOCOLATE PIE

**1 to 1½ cups fine chocolate wafer
   crumbs
¼ lb. melted butter
6 oz. semisweet chocolate
3 eggs
1½ tsp. rum
1 cup heavy whipping cream**

Mix together chocolate wafer crumbs and butter. Press into greased 9-inch pie pan. Melt chocolate. Cool slightly. Beat in 1 egg, 2 egg yolks, and rum. Beat whipping cream to soft peaks and fold into chocolate. Beat egg whites until stiff. Fold into chocolate. Fill pie shell and refrigerate 4 to 6 hours.

Serves 8   KATIE LORETTA

FALL LUNCH

*Ham-Cheese Chowder
*Tomato Salad
*Black Banana Bread
or
*Pecan Muffins

HAM-CHEESE CHOWDER

½ **cup coarsely shredded carrot**
¼ **cup chopped onion**
¼ **cup butter or margarine**
3 T. flour
4 cups milk
1½ **cups diced cooked ham**
½ **tsp. celery seed**
½ **tsp. Worcestershire sauce**
1 cup sharp processed American or
   cheddar cheese, cubed
snipped chives

In large saucepan cook carrot and onion in butter until tender but not brown. Blend in flour; add milk. Cook and stir until thickened and bubbly. Stir in diced ham, celery seed, and Worcestershire sauce. Heat through. Add cheese, stirring until melted. Garnish with snipped chives.

Serves 4   ELAINE MAIMONE

TOMATO SALAD

1 large can tomatoes
2 T. vinegar
2 tsp. sugar
1 T. butter
dash salt
1⅓ small pkg. lemon gelatin
1 onion, chopped
1 green pepper, chopped
1 cup celery, chopped
Topping:
    ½ cup sour cream
    ½ cup mayonnaise
    1 onion, chopped
    1 cucumber, diced

Cook tomatoes, vinegar, sugar, salt, and butter 5 minutes. Add lemon gelatin and cool. Fold in onions, pepper and celery. Mold.

Serves 12   MARY W. HARRELL

BLACK BANANA BREAD

2 over-ripe bananas
1 cup sugar
1 tsp. baking soda
⅛ tsp. salt
2 cups flour
2 eggs
¼ cup buttermilk or 2 oz. milk with
    1 T. vinegar
2 oz. vegetable oil

Blend bananas, sugar, soda and salt. Add flour and eggs in turn, blending well. Add oil and buttermilk. Mix well. Bake at 300 degrees for 1 hour. Makes 1 large loaf or 2 small ones.

Serves 12   RITA BUCHANAN

PECAN MUFFINS

½ cup butter
1¼ cups firmly packed brown sugar
2 eggs
1 tsp. baking soda
1 cup buttermilk
1 tsp. vanilla
½ tsp. salt
1¾ cups flour
¾ cup chopped pecans

Cream butter with sugar until fluffy. Add eggs one at a time. Dissolve baking soda in buttermilk; mix in vanilla and salt. Add alternately with flour. Mix in pecans. Line muffin tins and fill ¾ full with batter. Bake at 375 degrees for 15 to 20 minutes.

Yield: 1 dozen   NANCY L. WALSH

AFTER SCHOOL SNACKS

*Grandma's Gum Drop Cookies
*Bird Seed
*Whole Wheat Peanut Butter Cookies
*Butter Cookies
Fresh Fruit

GRANDMA'S GUM DROP COOKIES

2¼ cups brown sugar
3 eggs
1 T. water
2 cups flour
1 tsp. baking powder
¼ tsp. salt
1½ cups small gum drops (not black)
½ cup nuts

**(at Christmas, use red and green
gumdrops)**

Mix sugar, eggs and water well; add flour, baking
powder, salt; mix well, then add gum drops and nuts.
Spread on jelly-roll pan. Bake at 350 degrees until
light brown (20 minutes). Dust with powdered sugar.

KAREN SHANAHAN

BIRD SEED

Peanuts
Raisins
M & M's or
Semi-Sweet Morsels

Mix together equal portions of above in bowl.

THE COMMITTEE

134

WHOLE WHEAT
PEANUT BUTTER COOKIES

½ cup butter or margarine
½ cup peanut butter
½ cup sugar
½ cup brown sugar
1 egg
½ tsp. vanilla
1¼ cups whole wheat flour
½ tsp. baking powder
¾ tsp. baking soda
¼ tsp. salt

Cream margarine, peanut butter and sugars. Add egg and vanilla. Add flour, baking powder, baking soda and salt. Chill. Shape into balls and flatten with a fork. Bake on a greased cookie sheet 8 to 12 minutes at 375 degrees. (Note: if "sugar conscious," the total sugar can be reduced to ¹/₃ to ½ cup, very successfully.)

Yield: 4 dozen   MARCIA BALL

BUTTER COOKIES

¾ lb. butter
1½ cups sugar
2 tsp. vanilla
2 whole eggs (large or extra-large,
    not jumbo)
3½ cups flour
2½ tsp. baking powder

Cream butter with wooden spoon. Add sugar, vanilla and eggs. Mix flour and baking powder together. Add flour mixture to butter mixture. Use cookie press to shape. Bake on ungreased cookie sheet at 325 degrees to 350 degrees for 12 minutes.

Yield: 5 dozen   URSULA HLAVACEK

FAMILY DINNER

*Braised Short Ribs of Beef
*Potato Casserole
Buttered Green Beans
*Honey Glazed Carrots
*Open Pear Crunch Pie
Beaujolais or California Zinfandel

BRAISED SHORT RIBS OF BEEF

2 lbs. boneless short ribs of beef,
   well trimmed
½ cup flour
2 to 3 T. oil
1 medium onion, chopped
1 carrot, diced
1 stalk celery, diced
1 clove garlic, chopped fine
salt and pepper to taste
2 beef bouillon cubes
½ cup boiling water
½ cup Cabernet Sauvignon wine

Dredge meat with flour. Season. Brown on all sides in oil in Dutch oven. Add vegetables. Dissolve bouillon cubes in water. Add bouillon and wine to vegetables and meat. Cover and bake at 300 degrees for 2 to 3 hours, or until meat is very tender. If there is too much liquid, uncover during last 30 or 60 minutes of cooking time. Turn meat once to keep top from drying out.

Serves 3 to 4   JENNY PERRY

POTATO CASSEROLE

6 medium potatoes
¼ cup butter
1 can cream of mushroom soup
1½ cups cheddar cheese, grated
1 pint sour cream
⅓ cup chopped onion
1 cup corn flake crumbs
3 T. melted butter
salt to taste

Cook potatoes until tender, about 25 minutes. Cool, peel and grate. In large saucepan, heat butter with soup. Blend in cheese, add salt to taste, sour cream and onions. Stir in potatoes. Place in 2½-quart buttered casserole. Mix corn flake crumbs and melted butter. Place on top of casserole. Bake at 350 degrees for 45 minutes.

Serves 6   MARY ANNE GREINER

HONEY GLAZED CARROTS

6 medium carrots
1 cup water
½ tsp. salt
2 T. butter
½ tsp. dried mint leaves
2 T. brown sugar
1 T. honey
dash of salt

Clean and slice carrots. Cook with salt in boiling water until tender, about 20 to 25 minutes. Drain. Melt butter and stir in mint leaves. Add carrots, sugar, honey and salt and cook until well-glazed, turning constantly.

Serves 4   PAULA KAPPOS

OPEN PEAR CRUNCH PIE

1 basic-pastry pie shell
¼ cup apricot jam
1 T. water
5 pears
½ cup sugar
3 T. lemon juice
1 T. grated lemon rind
½ cup brown sugar
1 tsp. cinnamon
½ tsp. nutmeg
¼ tsp. ginger
⅓ cup butter
½ cup flour
2 T. toasted sesame seeds (optional)

Preheat oven to 425 degrees. Bake pie shell for 8 to 10 minutes. Lower heat to 400 degrees. Heat jam and water until of spreadable consistency and brush over pie shell. Peel, core and slice pears. Mix with sugar, lemon peel, and juice. Arrange in pie shell. Combine brown sugar, flour, butter, spices and sesame seeds, mixing with fingertips until the consistency of coarse meal. Spread over pears. Bake for 45 minutes until pears are tender. Serve with softly whipped cream.

Serves 6 to 8   KATHERINE MAVEC

FRIDAY NIGHT SUPPER

*Bob's Favorite Chopped Sirloin
Buttered Spinach
Mashed Potatoes
*Cherry Ice Cream Dessert
California Pinot Noir or Monthelie

BOB'S FAVORITE CHOPPED SIRLOIN

1 lb. ground sirloin
1 egg
1 sprig parsley, chopped
salt, pepper, garlic salt to taste
2 oz. butter
3 oz. Burgundy wine
6 large mushrooms, sliced
1 green pepper, sliced
1-8 oz. can tomato puree
grated Parmesan cheese

Mix together ground sirloin, egg, chopped parsley and seasonings. Shape into 2 large patties and saute in butter until browned on both sides. Pour in wine and allow patties to cook in wine for 5 minutes, turning a few times. Add mushrooms and green pepper. When these are par-cooked, add tomato puree then simmer 15 to 20 minutes. Remove from pan, place in casserole, sprinkle with Parmesan cheese and brown under broiler. Serve immediately.

Serves 2   EUNICE PODIS WEISKOPF

CHERRY ICE CREAM DESSERT

1 cup flour
1 cup sugar
1 tsp. baking soda
dash salt
1 egg
1-16 oz. can tart, pitted cherries,
    drained (reserve juice for sauce)
1 tsp. butter or margarine
¼ cup brown sugar
¼ cup nuts, chopped

Mix flour, sugar, soda and salt. Make hole in center; add cherries and egg. Mix well. Melt 1 tsp. butter in an 8 x 8-inch pan then add mixture. Sprinkle with brown sugar and nuts. Bake at 325 degrees for 45 minutes. Cut in squares and cool. Top each square with vanilla ice cream and warm sauce just before serving.

SAUCE

1 cup cherry juice
1 cup sugar
½ tsp. almond extract
1 tsp. butter or margarine
1 T. flour

Combine all ingredients and cook, stirring until thickened.

Serves 6   SHARON FREIMUTH

"BEATRICE AND BENEDICT"

Hot Cocoa
*Breakfast Egg Casserole
*Raisin Bran Bread
*Peach Clafouti

BREAKFAST EGG CASSEROLE

12 eggs, beaten
2 cans cheddar cheese soup
4 tsp. dry mustard
8 slices fresh bread, shredded
2 lbs. sausage, browned and drained
melted butter

Combine eggs and soup. Add mustard. Add shredded bread and combine well. Spread in greased 9 x 13-inch pan. Sprinkle sausage, then melted butter on top. Chill overnight. Bake at 350 degrees for 30 minutes.

Serves 12   PAULA KAPPOS

RAISIN BRAN BREAD

1 cup whole wheat flour
1¼ cups all-purpose flour
2¼ tsp. baking powder
1 tsp. salt
½ cup shortening
¾ cup granulated sugar
2 eggs
1 cup 100% Bran or All Bran cereal
¾ cup raisins
½ cup milk

Sift together first 4 ingredients. Beat shortening and sugar until creamy. Add eggs and beat until light and fluffy. Stir in cereal and raisins. Alternately add milk and flour mixture. Turn into greased 5 x 9-inch loaf pan. Bake in a preheated 350 degree oven approximately 1 hour. Cool in pan 10 minutes then remove to rack to cool completely.

Serves 12   SARA HAWK

PEACH CLAFOUTI

3 T. sugar
4½ cups sliced, peeled peaches
1½ cups milk
1½ cups cream
5 eggs
6 T. flour
pinch of salt
4 T. sugar
1½ tsp. vanilla
confectioners' sugar

Sprinkle a well-buttered, 2-quart, shallow, oval baking dish with 3 T. sugar. Evenly distribute sliced peaches over sugared baking dish. In mixer or blender combine milk, cream, eggs, flour, and pinch of salt. Mix briefly about 2 minutes. Add 4 T. sugar and vanilla and blend very briefly. Pour mixture over fruit. Bake in preheated 375 degree oven for 45 to 50 minutes until puffed and golden. Sprinkle with sifted confectioners' sugar and serve warm.

Serves 12   SUSAN LEVINE

"RODEO"

*Bobbie's Corn-Pumpkin Chowder
Hamburgers 'n Hot Dogs
*Hot Dog Relish
Tossed Salad
*Best French Vanilla Ice Cream
Hot Fudge Sauce

BOBBIE'S CORN-PUMPKIN CHOWDER

**2 large yellow onions, thinly sliced
2 T. butter
1½ tsp. flour
1 can condensed chicken broth, undiluted
1 lb. can pumpkin
1-17 oz. can cream-style corn
3 cups milk
1 cup light cream
1 tsp. salt
⅛ tsp. pepper
¼ tsp. ginger
¼ tsp. nutmeg
¼ tsp. coriander
2 tsp. parsley**

In a 6-quart dutch oven, saute onions in butter about 10 minutes. Remove from heat and stir in flour, then add broth. Simmer, covered for 10 minutes. Remove and puree in food processor. Return to pan and add pumpkin, corn, milk, cream and seasonings. Simmer slowly 20 to 25 minutes covered.

Serves 10   DORI HAAS

HOT DOG RELISH

3 lbs. green tomatoes
4 red apples
3 sweet red peppers
4 onions
1½ T. coarse salt
1½ tsp. pepper
1½ tsp. cinnamon
¾ tsp. ground cloves
2½ cups sugar
2 cups cider vinegar

Stem and quarter tomatoes, apples, peppers and onions. Put through food chopper using coarse blade. Combine remaining ingredients and bring to a boil in large kettle. Add chopped vegetables and simmer uncovered about 30 minutes or until thick, stirring occasionally. Ladle into hot sterile jars and seal immediately.

Makes about 7 pints   GINNA HERMANN

BEST FRENCH VANILLA
ICE CREAM

6 egg yolks
1½ cups sugar
¼ tsp. salt
4 tsp. vanilla
4 cups heavy cream
2 cups half-and-half cream
4 T. unsalted butter, melted

Beat egg yolks until thickened. Add sugar, salt and vanilla. Mix heavy cream with half-and-half. Add to egg mixture. Stir in butter. Chill well. Freeze in ice cream freezer using crushed ice.

Serves 8 to 10   MRS. S. TIMOTHY KILTY

"THE BEGGAR'S OPERA"

*Cream of Vegetable Soup
*Ham Loaf
*Pineapple Casserole
*Fluffy White Cake with
*Seven Minute Icing
German Rhine Spatlese

CREAM OF VEGETABLE SOUP

2 T. butter
1 clove garlic, chopped
1 medium onion, sliced
¼ head cauliflower
2 carrots, sliced
2 stalks celery, sliced
6 asparagus stalks, cut into 1-inch
   pieces
1 leek, chopped
1 large potato, peeled and chopped
1 cup spinach, chopped
salt and pepper
4 cups chicken or veal stock
Tabasco
1 cup heavy cream
1 T. chopped parsley
1 T. grated Parmesan

In large soup pot, melt butter and saute onion and garlic for several minutes. Prepare vegetables. Add all but spinach to pot and cook 5 minutes. Add stock and simmer for 20 minutes. Add spinach and simmer 10 minutes more. Mix cream and flour with a little soup broth until smooth. Pour slowly into the soup, stirring constantly. Simmer until slightly thickened. Garnish with parsley and cheese.

Serves 6 to 8   JENNIFER LANGSTON

HAM LOAF

1 lb. ground ham
1 lb. ground pork
1 egg, beaten
¾ cup milk
1 cup crushed graham crackers
¾ cup brown sugar
1½ tsp. ground mustard
½ can tomato soup
¼ cup vinegar (any kind)

Mix meat, egg, milk and crushed graham crackers together. Shape into a loaf and place in baking dish. Mix brown sugar and dry mustard; add tomato soup and vinegar. Mix and heat. Pour sauce over loaf and bake at 350 degrees for 1 hour. Baste once if needed.

Serves 8 to 10   MRS. PAUL E. WESTLAKE

PINEAPPLE CASSEROLE

¼ lb. butter, melted
½ cup sugar
1 T. flour
salt
2 beaten eggs
1-20 oz. can crushed pineapple and
   juice
5 slices broken bread

Mix all ingredients except the bread. Then add the bread. Bake in a 1-quart casserole at 325 degrees for 45 minutes or until golden brown.

Serves 6 to 8   SARA HAWK

FLUFFY WHITE CAKE

2⅓ cups all-purpose flour
2 cups sugar
4 tsp. baking powder
1 tsp. salt
1½ cups milk
⅔ cup shortening
5 egg whites, unbeaten
1 tsp. almond flavoring

Combine and blend in large mixer bowl flour, sugar, salt and baking powder. Add milk and shortening. Beat two minutes at medium speed. Add egg whites and flavoring. Beat two minutes more. Pour into two greased and floured 9-inch layer pans or a 9 x 13-inch pan. Bake at 375 degrees 30 to 35 minutes in layers; 35 to 40 minutes in 9 x 13-inch pan. When cool, frost with Seven Minute Icing.

SEVEN MINUTE ICING

2 egg whites
1½ cups sugar
½ cup water
1 T. white corn syrup
½ tsp. salt
1 tsp. vanilla

In double boiler, combine all ingredients except vanilla. With electric mixer at high speed, beat 1 minute; then place over rapidly boiling water and beat until mixer forms peaks when beater is raised (can take longer than 7 minutes). Remove from boiling water and transfer into large mixing bowl. Add vanilla and continue beating until thick enough to spread.

Serves 10 to 12   DIANNE VOGT

BOUNTIFUL BRUNCH

*Chili Egg Puff
Fresh Fruit Salad with
*Halle's Dressing
*Bran Muffins
*"Midnight Special" Poppyseed Cake

CHILI EGG PUFF

10 eggs
½ cup unsifted flour
1 tsp. baking powder
½ tsp. salt
**1-16 oz. carton of small-curd
    creamed cottage cheese**
1 lb. Jack cheese, shredded
½ cup butter, melted
2-4 oz. cans diced green chiles

In a large bowl, beat eggs until light and lemon colored. Add flour, baking powder, salt, cottage cheese, Jack cheese and melted butter. Blend until smooth. Stir in chiles. Pour mixture into a well-buttered 9 x 13-inch baking dish. Bake at 350 degrees for 35 minutes or until top is browned. (May be made night before and refrigerated until ready to bake.)

Serves 10 to 12   JANICE THOMPSON

149

HALLE'S TEA ROOM
FLUFFY FRUIT DRESSING

1 cup unsweetened pineapple juice
½ cup lemon juice
3 eggs, beaten
1 cup granulated sugar
2 cups whipping cream

Mix fruit juices. Add eggs and sugar. Cook in double boiler until thickened. Cool. Whip cream and fold into cooled mixture.

JANE BROOKE

BRAN MUFFINS

2 cups bran buds
2 cups oatmeal
2 cups shredded wheat
4 eggs
3 cups sugar
1 tsp. salt
1 cup vegetable oil
4 cups buttermilk
5 tsp. baking soda
5 cups flour
2 cups nuts, raisins, or dates (optional)
2 cups boiling water (see directions)

Mix cereals together. Beat eggs, sugar, salt and oil together. Then add to cereal. Combine soda with flour and add to cereal mixture alternately with buttermilk. Add nuts, raisins or dates. (If you do not want to bake right away, pour 2 cups boiling water over batter, cover and store in refrigerator up to 2 weeks. If stored, stir mixture before spooning in tins.) Bake at 400 degrees for 20 minutes.

Yield: 5 dozen

INEZ DONOFRIO

"MIDNIGHT SPECIAL" POPPY SEED CAKE

1 cup poppy seed
1½ cups milk
⅓ cup honey
¼ cup water
1 cup softened butter or margarine
1½ cups sugar
4 egg yolks
1 cup sour cream
1 tsp. vanilla
2½ cups sifted flour
1 tsp. baking soda
½ tsp. salt
4 stiffly beaten egg whites

Soak poppy seeds in milk overnight. Next day, drain off excess milk. In a 1-quart saucepan cook poppy seeds with honey and water 3 minutes. Cool. Cream butter and sugar until soft and fluffy. Add cooled poppy seed mixture. Add egg yolks one at a time beating well after each addition. Blend in sour cream and vanilla. Sift together flour, soda and salt. Gradually add to poppy seed mixture, beating well after each addition. Carefully fold in stiffly beaten egg whites. Pour batter into lightly greased and floured 10-inch tube pan. Bake in preheated 350 degree oven 1 hour 15 minutes or until tester comes out clean. Cool in pan at least 5 minutes. Remove and cool on a wire rack. Sprinkle with powdered sugar.

Serves 12 to 16   IRVING NATHANSON
                          THE CLEVELAND ORCHESTRA

"BIRD QUARTET"

*Parmesan Oven-Fried Chicken
*Pasta with Broccoli
Italian Rolls
*Apricot Coconut Balls or
*Cheesecake Dreams
Pinot Grigio or Sassella

PARMESAN OVEN-FRIED CHICKEN

2½ to 3 lbs. chicken, cut up
¾ cup fine bread crumbs
¼ cup grated Parmesan
¼ cup chopped, blanched almonds
½ cup unsalted butter
2 T. parsley, minced
1 tsp. salt
¾ tsp. garlic powder
¼ tsp. thyme
⅛ tsp. pepper

Preheat oven to 375 degrees. Combine crumbs, cheese and almonds in a pie pan and set aside. Blend softened butter, parsley and seasonings and spread over chicken. Roll pieces in crumb mixture coating well. Place chicken, skin side up, in ungreased 9 x 13-inch pan. Bake uncovered, without turning, at 375 degrees for 55 to 65 minutes or until golden brown.

Serves 4   KATHY COQUILLETTE

PASTA WITH BROCCOLI

1 bunch broccoli
4 T. olive oil
4 T. butter
2 T. coarsely chopped garlic
hot pepper flakes (optional) or freshly ground black pepper to taste
1 to 1½ cups water
½ lb. linguine or spaghettini broken into 2-inch lengths
1 tomato, chopped

Cut broccoli into florets and quarter stalks. Peel stems off, then cut into 2-inch lengths. Heat oil and butter in large skillet. Add garlic and pepper. When oil is hot add broccoli, one cup of water, and uncooked pasta. Mix well. Add tomatoes. Cover and cook over medium heat about 10 minutes. Mix often, adding more water if necessary, so pasta does not stick.

Serves 4   JENNIFER LANGSTON

APRICOT COCONUT BALLS

1½ cups dried apricots ground in small pieces
2 cups shredded coconut
⅔ cup sweetened condensed milk
confectioners' sugar

Combine apricots and coconut. Add milk and blend. Shape into small balls and roll in sugar. Let stand till firm.

KAREN SHANAHAN

CHEESECAKE DREAMS

⅓ cup firmly packed light-brown
    sugar
1 cup all-purpose flour
½ cup chopped walnuts
⅓ cup melted margarine
1-8 oz. pkg. cream cheese, softened
¼ cup sugar
1 egg
2 T. milk
1 T. lemon juice
1 tsp. vanilla

Preheat oven to 350 degrees. Grease an 8 x 8-inch baking pan. In small bowl, mix first three ingredients. Stir in melted margarine until well blended. Set aside ⅓ cup crumbs and pat rest in pan. Bake 12 to 15 minutes. In small bowl, at medium speed, beat cream cheese and sugar until smooth. Beat in remaining ingredients. Pour over baked crust. Sprinkle on remaining crumbs. Bake 25 minutes more until set. Cool on rack. Cut into 2-inch squares, then cut diagonally in half.

Yield: 32   TORY WILLOUGHBY

"RIGOLETTO"

*Special Company Spaghetti
Garlic Bread
*Lemonade Jello
Spumoni
*Biscotti
Chianti Classico or Gattinara

SPECIAL COMPANY SPAGHETTI

3 garlic cloves, minced
1 onion, chopped
¼ cup olive oil
3 large tomatoes, peeled and chopped
1-8 oz. can tomato sauce
1 tsp. salt
1 tsp. sugar
pinch of pepper
½ tsp. Italian seasoning
20 raw shrimp, peeled and deveined
1-7 oz. can minced clams
½ to 1 lb. spaghetti, cooked

Saute garlic and onion in oil for about 5 minutes. Add tomato, tomato sauce and seasonings. Cook and simmer for one hour. Add shrimp and simmer uncovered for 5 minutes. Add clams and simmer an additional 5 minutes. Pour sauce over spaghetti and serve immediately.

Serves 4   SHIRLEY SCHOENBERGER

LEMONADE JELLO

1-6 oz. box of lemon gelatin
2 cups boiling water
1-12 oz. can of frozen lemonade
9 oz. frozen "whipped" topping

Dissolve gelatin in boiling water. Add lemonade and stir. Whisk in whipped topping. Pour into 6-cup mold and refrigerate overnight. To serve, unmold on a platter and garnish with fresh fruit, cherry tomatoes or olives. (This separates; top is clear and bottom is creamy.)

Serves 16   CAROLYN ROSS

BISCOTTI (ANISE TOAST)

1¼ cups sugar
1½ sticks of butter or margarine
3 eggs
¼ cup milk
3 T. crushed anise seed
3½ cups unsifted flour
3 tsp. baking powder

Cream butter and sugar; add eggs, milk and crushed anise seed. Slowly add flour and baking powder. Make two long strips of dough on a cookie sheet. Bake at 375 degrees for 30 minutes. Remove and allow to cool slightly. Cut strips in 1-inch pieces. Return slices to cookie sheet and bake at 425 degrees for about 10 minutes or until brown.

MRS. J.A. WILLIAMS, JR.

"SUMMERTIME"

*Flank Steak
Skewered Tomatoes, Mushrooms and Onions
Breadsticks
*Six Threes Ice Cream
*Iowa Brownies
California Cabernet or Côtes du Rhône

FLANK STEAK

1 cup salad oil
½ cup soy sauce
¼ cup honey
½ tsp. garlic powder
½ tsp. ginger (optional)
1 T. minced, dried onion
1½ lbs. flank steak

Combine ingredients. Pour over the flank steak and marinate overnight. Broil or grill steak. Baste with the marinade while cooking. To serve, slice on an angle.

Serves 4   CAROLYN ROSS

SIX THREES ICE CREAM

3 bananas, mashed
juice of 3 oranges
juice of 3 lemons
3 cups sugar
3 cups whipping cream
3 cups milk

Mix all ingredients together, stir. Pour into an electric ice cream freezer and freeze.

Yield: 1 gallon   MARY L. MOORE

IOWA BROWNIES

1 stick margarine
1 cup sugar
1-1 lb. can Hershey's syrup
4 eggs
1 cup flour
1 cup chopped nuts

Combine all ingredients together. Pour into 9 x 13-inch pan. Bake at 350 degrees for 30 minutes. These will look gooey when you take them out of the oven. Pour icing over baked brownies.

ICING

1 stick margarine
1½ cups sugar
⅓ cup evaporated milk
½ cup chocolate chips

Boil all ingredients except chocolate chips for 1 minute, then add chocolate chips.

KAREN SHANAHAN

"LE PAUVRE MATELOT"

*"Hello Mom" Casserole
*Cranberry Jello Salad
*Lazy Daisy Cake
Côtes du Rhône

"HELLO MOM" CASSEROLE

1-5 oz. pkg. egg noodles
3 T. butter
3 T. flour
1½ cups milk
salt and pepper to taste
1 medium can tuna or crabmeat
1 pkg. or jar pimento cheese
3 hard-cooked eggs
12 ripe olives
1 small can mushrooms
1 green pepper, chopped fine
buttered crumbs

Cook noodles in boiling water until tender. Drain. Make white sauce of butter, flour, milk, salt, and pepper. Combine all ingredients. Pour into buttered baking dish, top with buttered crumbs and bake at 350 degrees for 45 minutes.

Serves 6 to 8   DEDE BAKER

CRANBERRY JELLO SALAD

1-6 oz. pkg. raspberry jello
1 cup hot water
1 can jellied cranberry sauce
1 cup sour cream
2 cups nuts, chopped

Dissolve jello in hot water and cool. Beat sour cream and cranberry sauce until well blended; then add nuts. Combine mixture with jello and refrigerate.

Serves 11 to 12   MARY L. MOORE

LAZY DAISY CAKE

2 eggs
1 cup flour
1 cup sugar
1 tsp. baking powder
½ tsp. salt
1 tsp. vanilla
½ cup milk
4 T. unsalted butter

Beat eggs well, add flour, sugar, baking powder, salt, vanilla. Bring milk to a boil, melt butter in milk. Add to first mixture. Pour into greased 9 x 9-inch cake pan. Bake at 350 degrees for 25 minutes.

FROSTING

3 T. melted butter
5 T. brown sugar
½ cup coconut
2 T. milk

Make frosting by combining melted butter, brown sugar, coconut and milk. Spread on cake. Broil in oven until light brown.

KATHY COQUILLETTE

"MIRACULOUS MANDARIN"

*Oriental Chicken Stir-Fry or
*Oriental Pork Platter
Rice
*Chinese Chews
*Almond Cookies
St. Veran or California Pinot Noir

ORIENTAL CHICKEN STIR-FRY

¼ **cup oil**
3 **whole broiler-fryer chicken**
  breasts, boned, skinned and cut
  into 1-inch chunks
3 **cups broccoli florets**
1 **medium red pepper, cut into 1-**
  inch squares
½ **lb. mushrooms, sliced**
3 **T. thinly sliced scallions**
1 **cup chicken broth**
3 **T. dry sherry**
1 **T. cornstarch**
1 **T. soy sauce**
½ **tsp. liquid hot pepper sauce**
⅓ **cup cashew nuts**

In large skillet, preferably an iron one, or a wok, heat oil. Add chicken and cook over moderate heat for 5 minutes, stirring frequently, until chicken is white. Remove from wok. Place broccoli, red pepper, mushrooms and scallions in wok. Cook 3 minutes, stirring frequently. In a small bowl, mix chicken broth, sherry, cornstarch, soy sauce and liquid hot pepper. Return chicken to wok along with chicken broth mixture. Cook, stirring constantly, 5 minutes until sauce thickens slightly. Sprinkle with cashew nuts.

Serves 6   REGINA DAILY

ORIENTAL PORK PLATTER

12 slices thin cooked pork
¼ cup soy sauce
½ cup sherry
3 T. vegetable oil
2 medium onions, sliced
2 medium green peppers, diced
2 yellow squash, sliced
½ lb. fresh mushrooms, sliced
1½ cups water
1 tsp. instant chicken broth
2 tsp. salt
1-8 oz. can water chestnuts, sliced
2 T. cornstarch
¼ cup cold water

Marinate pork in soy sauce and sherry for several hours. Heat oil in frying pan. Brown pork, remove and keep warm in some heated marinade. Saute onion; add green pepper and squash and saute for 2 minutes. Add mushrooms, marinade, chicken broth, water chestnuts, salt and water and heat until vegetables are crisp - tender. Mix cornstarch with ¼ cup water and add to skillet. Heat until thickened.

Serves 4 to 6   KATHLEEN GRIFFIN

CHINESE CHEWS

2 cups flour
1 cup butter
1 cup brown sugar
1½ cups brown sugar
2 T. flour
¼ tsp. salt
1 cup chopped pecans
2 eggs
1 tsp. vanilla
½ tsp. baking powder

Mix first 3 ingredients to crumbs and press into shallow 9 x 9-inch pan. Bake at 300 degrees for 10 minutes. Beat together all remaining ingredients and spread over crust. Bake again at 300 degrees for 40 minutes or until light brown. Inside should be fairly moist when removed from oven. Cool and cut into squares.

Yield: 2 dozen   DIANE GILL

ALMOND COOKIES

4 oz. soft almond paste
4 oz. unsalted butter, softened
½ c. sugar
¼ tsp. salt
½ tsp. baking powder
¾ c. flour
¼ tsp. almond extract
1 egg white

Mix together sugar and almond paste. Add softened butter, 2 T. at a time, beating well after each addition. Beat in egg white. Add almond extract. Sift dry ingredients and add. Drop by teaspoonfuls onto greased cookie sheet. Bake at 375 degrees for 10 to 12 minutes.

Yield: 3 dozen   VIRGINIA BARBATO

"LE BOEUF SUR LE TOIT"

*Deviled Flank Steak
Steak Fries
*Broccoli-Onion Deluxe
*Chocolate Cherry Cake
Beaujolais or Côtes du Rhône

DEVILED FLANK STEAK

1½ to 2 lbs. flank steak
1 garlic clove
1 tsp. salt
1 tsp. rosemary
½ tsp. ginger
½ cup prepared mustard
2 T. soy sauce

Preheat oven to broil. Score meat on both sides. Mash garlic, salt, spices with spoon back to make paste. Stir in mustard and soy sauce. Spread ½ mixture on one side of steak. Broil on this side for 5 minutes. Turn and spread mixture on other side. Broil 5 minutes. Cut against grain into thin slices. Serve hot or cold.

Serves 4 to 6   ELIZABETH B. NUECHTERLEIN

BROCCOLI-ONION DELUXE

1 lb. broccoli (or 1-10 oz. pkg. frozen
  cut broccoli)
2 cups frozen whole small pearl
  onions
4 T. butter or margarine
2 T. flour
¼ tsp. salt
dash pepper
1 cup milk
1-3 oz. pkg. cream cheese
2 oz. cheddar cheese, grated
1 cup soft bread crumbs

Cut broccoli into 1-inch pieces. Cook in boiling, salted water. (Cook frozen broccoli by package directions.) Drain. Cook onions in boiling salted water. Drain. In saucepan, melt 2 T. butter. Blend in flour, salt and pepper. Add milk. Cook, stirring until thick and bubbly. Reduce heat and stir in cream cheese until smooth. Place vegetables in 1½-quart casserole. Pour sauce over, mix lightly. Top with cheddar cheese. Melt 2 T. butter and toss with bread crumbs. Cover and bake at 350 degrees for 30 minutes. Remove lid. Sprinkle crumbs over top. Bake 15 to 30 minutes more until heated through.

Serves 6   MEREDITH BASS

CHOCOLATE CHERRY CAKE

1 box devil's food cake mix
1-21 oz. can cherry pie filling
2 large eggs, beaten
1 tsp. almond extract

Preheat oven to 350 degrees. Combine all cake ingredients and stir until well mixed. Pour into greased and floured 9 x 13-inch pan and bake 25 to 30 minutes or until toothpick inserted in center comes out dry. Frost while warm.

FROSTING

1 cup sugar
5 T. butter
⅓ cup milk
1 cup chocolate chips

Combine sugar, butter and milk in saucepan. Bring to boil for 1 minute. Remove from heat and stir in chocolate chips. Stir until smooth and slightly thick. Pour over warm cake.

CAROLYN ROSS

INDEX

BACH COOKBOOKS
Severance Hall
Cleveland, Ohio 44106

Make checks payable to:
BACH COOKBOOKS

Please send me:

_____ copies of **BACH'S LUNCH** @ **$6.95**
                (Picnic and Patio Classics) $ _____

_____ copies of **BACH FOR MORE** @ **$6.95**
                (Fireside Classics) $ _____

_____ copies of **BACH FOR AN ENCORE** @ **$6.95**
                (Menu Classics) $ _____

Plus **$1.50** postage and handling per book $ _____

For Ohio delivery please add **$.46** tax per book $ _____

Total enclosed $ _____

Name _____

Street _____

City _____ State _____ Zip _____
                      Please Print

All proceeds from the sale of these cookbooks are for
the benefit of The Cleveland Orchestra.

BACH COOKBOOKS
Severance Hall
Cleveland, Ohio 44106

Make checks payable to:
BACH COOKBOOKS

Please send me:

_____ copies of **BACH'S LUNCH** @ **$6.95**
                (Picnic and Patio Classics) $ _____

_____ copies of **BACH FOR MORE** @ **$6.95**
                (Fireside Classics) $ _____

_____ copies of **BACH FOR AN ENCORE** @ **$6.95**
                (Menu Classics) $ _____

Plus **$1.50** postage and handling per book $ _____

For Ohio delivery please add **$.46** tax per book $ _____

Total enclosed $ _____

Name _____

Street _____

City _____ State _____ Zip _____
                      Please Print

All proceeds from the sale of these cookbooks are for
the benefit of The Cleveland Orchestra.